本书的出版得到

国家重点文物保护专项补助经费资助

*

项目发掘经费承蒙以下基金会资助：

瑞士和列支敦士登国外考古学研究基金会

瑞士国家科学基金会

The publication of this volume was supported by the

Subsidy Fund for the Protection of Key Cultural Heritage in China

This excavation was funded by the following organisations:

Schweizerisch Liechtensteinische Stiftung für Archäologische Forschungen im Ausland (SLSA)

Swiss National Science Foundation

临朐白龙寺遗址发掘报告

山东省文物考古研究所
苏黎世大学东亚美术史系 编著
山东临朐山旺古生物化石博物馆

文物出版社

图书在版编目（CIP）数据

临朐白龙寺遗址发掘报告/山东省文物考古研究所，苏黎世大学东亚美术史系，山东临朐山旺古生物化石博物馆编著. —北京：文物出版社，2015.12

ISBN 978-7-5010-4414-6

Ⅰ. ①临…　Ⅱ. ①山…　②瑞…　③山…　Ⅲ. ①佛教－宗教建筑－文化遗址－发掘报告－临朐县　Ⅳ. ①K878.65

中国版本图书馆CIP数据核字(2015)第246012号

临 朐 白 龙 寺 遗 址 发 掘 报 告

编　　著：山东省文物考古研究所
　　　　　苏黎世大学东亚美术史系
　　　　　山东临朐山旺古生物化石博物馆

责任编辑：秦　彧
责任印制：梁秋卉

出版发行：文物出版社
地　　址：北京市东直门内北小街2号楼
邮　　编：100007
网　　址：http://www.wenwu.com
邮　　箱：web@wenwu.com
制版印刷：北京荣宝燕泰印务有限公司
经　　销：新华书店
开　　本：889mm×1194mm　　1/16
印　　张：14.75　　插页：3
版　　次：2015年12月第1版
印　　次：2015年12月第1次印刷
书　　号：ISBN 978-7-5010-4414-6
定　　价：210.00元

White Dragon Temple Site in Linqu County

by

Shandong Provincial Institute of Cultural Relics and Archaeology

Department of East Asian Art History, Zurich University

Shanwang Fossils Museum in Linqu County, Shandong Province

Cultural Relics Press

佟佩华（中国）　倪克鲁（瑞士）　李振光（中国）　主编

Tong Peihua (China) , Lukas Nickel (Switzerland) , Li Zhenguang (China)

序

谢治秀

山东是中华古代文明的重要发祥地之一。山东省的考古工作，自1928年济南章丘龙山镇发现城子崖龙山文化遗址，经过80余年的艰苦探索，逐步建立起独具特征的区域性考古学文化发展谱系。最早的沂源猿人距今40万年左右，新泰乌珠台人距今5～2万年左右，历经沂沭河流域和汶泗河流域的细石器文化遗存、后李文化、北辛文化、大汶口文化、龙山文化和岳石文化，进入历史文化时期。这一文化谱系每个阶段的连接较为紧密，文化传统的演变也一脉相承。

20世纪70年代以来山东相继出土了几批北朝时期重要的佛教造像：鲁北博兴、阳信、无棣、惠民、邹平和滨州等地区出土以铜造像为主体的佛教造像近300尊；诸城发现300余件佛教造像和100余件寺院建筑构件；临朐明道寺、白龙寺佛教建筑遗址发现300余尊佛教造像；青州龙兴寺遗址清理了一个佛教造像窖藏，发现北魏至北宋时期造像400余尊，被誉为"中国20世纪同敦煌石窟、安阳殷墟、临潼秦兵马俑一样，屈指可数的几个重要考古发现之一"。这些造像的出土，为研究佛教在中国的传播和发展，北朝时期佛教造像的断代、雕塑绘画艺术的演进等课题提供了极其珍贵的物质文化资料。

临朐与青州南北相邻，同属古青州版图核心区。临朐明道寺、大佛寺和白龙寺等遗址出土的佛教造像，雕刻精美，其年代以北朝为主。与青州龙兴寺、博兴龙华寺和诸城佛教造像风格相似，同属"青州风格"。临朐出土的佛教造像以纪年铭刻为重要特色，其中明道寺出土有年号的造像13件，用干支者4件；白龙寺遗址出土有年号的造像5件。这些具有年号和干支的佛教造像弥补了青州、诸城造像鲜有纪年的不足，为青州地区佛教造像分期断代提供了年代学依据。

2003年和2004年，经中国政府批准，由中国山东省文物考古研究所和瑞士苏黎世大学东亚美术史系共同组织了临朐白龙寺遗址的发掘。经过数年的努力，中、瑞双方考古学者完成了资料整理和报告编写工作，现在正式出版馈赠给学术界，这是一件值得庆贺的事情。这些发掘以及报告的出版，是中国和瑞士两国在文物考古领域的第一个合作项目。在合作期间，中、瑞学者以全新的文化遗产保护理念，实事求是的科学精神，勇于吃苦的工作态度，积极坦诚的交流方式，保证了合作项目的顺利进行，双方对此表示满意。当地百姓对于瑞士学者为中国文化遗产保护，顶风雨、冒酷暑的忘我精神所感动，无不称赞。

在合作发掘过程中，中、瑞两国政府和相关部门都给予了极大的支持。瑞士和列支敦士登国外考古学研究基金会、瑞士国家科学基金会给予了经济上的资助，山东省文物考古研究所提供了出版经费，我代表山东省文化厅表示诚挚的感谢。期望在今后的日子里，我们有更多新的合作。

Preface

Xie Zhixiu

Shandong area is one of the origins of Chinese ancient civilization. Archaeological research in Shandong Province began in the year 1928 when the first Longshan Culture site was discovered in Longshan village 龙山镇, Zhangqiu city. Now, after 80 years of exploration, the local archaeological past has been gradually reconstructed. It starts with the ape-man of Yiyuan 沂源 dating back to 400,000 years ago, and the Xintai Wuzhutai 新泰乌珠台 homo sapiens from 50 to 20, 000 years ago, followed by the Microlithic culture in the Yishu 沂沭 and Wensi 汶泗 river basins, the Houli 后李 culture, the Beixin 北辛 culture, the Dawenkou 大汶口 culture, the Longshan 龙山 culture and the Yueshi 岳石 culture, down to the historic period. Every stage of this development is closely connected to the next and the cultural traditions were handed down in one continuous line.

Since the 1970s, several groups of Buddhist sculptures were excavated in Shandong province: Boxing 博兴, Yangxin 阳信, Wudi 无棣, Huimin 惠民, Zouping 邹平 and Binzhou 滨州 in western Shandong yielded about 300 Buddhist sculptures, mainly composed of bronze statues. Nearly the same number of Buddhist sculptures and many building components were found in Zhucheng 诸城. The Mingdao Temple site 明道寺 in Linqu 临朐 and the Buddhist site in Xiao Shijiazhuang 小时家庄 also yielded a large number of sculptures. A pit was discovered in Longxing Temple 龙兴寺 in Qingzhou 青州, containing around 400 Buddhist sculptures dating from the Northern Wei to the Northern Song dynasty. The excavation of the Longxing Temple site was honoured as "one of the most important archaeological discoveries in 20th century AD China", together with the Dunhuang Grottoes, the Ruins of the Shang Dynasty city Anyang, and the Terracotta Warriors. The discoveries provided extremely valuable material for research on the spread of Buddhism in China, the dating of Buddhist sculptures of the Northern Dynasties, and the stylistic evolution of sculpture of this period.

Linqu and Qingzhou are today neighbouring cities and counties, but traditionally they were both part of ancient Qingzhou region. The Buddhist sculptures excavated from Linqu sites such as the Mingdao Temple, the Dafo Temple 大佛寺, and the temple site at Xiao Shijiazhuang are exquisitely made, and most of them date back to the Northern Dynasties. Stylistically these sculptures are comparable to the ones from Longxing Temple in Qingzhou, Longhua Temple 龙华寺 in Boxing, and temples in Zhucheng, presenting what is often called the 'Qingzhou Style'. In addition, many Buddhist sculptures found in Lingqu county bear dated inscriptions. Mingdao Temple yielded 13 sculptures bearing reign names, and four that are inscribed with cyclical characters. Five dated sculptures were excavated in the Xiao Shijiazhuang site. These dated sculptures help establishing a chronology for the development of Buddhist sculpture in ancient Qingzhou region.

During 2003 and 2004, with the authorization of the Chinese government, the Archaeological Institute of Shandong Province and Zurich University conducted a joint excavation of the Xiao Shijiazhuang temple site in Linqu. Through years of writing and compiling, scholars from both sides completed an archaeological report. Officially publishing this report will provide a great contribution to academia. It is worth celebrating. The publication of the report marks the conclusion of the first archaeological project conducted by scholars from China and Switzerland together. During the work, scholars from the two countries practiced an all new concept of cultural heritage protection. Adopting a scientific spirit of dedicated hard work and constructive and honest communication, they made the project a smooth success. The Swiss team left a deep impression among the local population. The villagers appreciated the efforts of the foreigners who continuously endured wind and rain as well as heat and cold in order to help protecting Chinese cultural heritage.

The excavation received substantial support by both the Chinese and the Swiss governments. The Schweizerisch-Liechtensteinische Stiftung für Archäologische Forschungen im Ausland and the Swiss National Science Foundation provided financial support during the excavation works. The Archaeological Institute of Shandong Province financed the publication of the report. On behalf of the Culture Office of Shandong Province, I would like to sincerely thank them for their support and help. I strongly hope that this successful collaboration will initiate more joint projects and renewed cooperation in the future.

目　录

contents

插图目录

彩版目录

第一章 前言

山东省地处中国东部，黄河下游，东临渤海、黄海。山东地貌中部山地隆起，地势最高，东部及南部丘陵和缓起伏，北部及西部平原坦荡。规模最大的山地为东西横亘的泰、鲁、沂山地，其中泰山海拔1532米，鲁山海拔1108米，沂山海拔1031米。河流水系受地貌格局的直接影响，以山地为中心，向四周流淌，其中淄河、弥河、潍河等向北流入渤海（图一）。临朐县小时家庄佛教遗址位于鲁山和沂山之间的深山峡谷中，弥河的支流从遗址南边流过，形成了一个临水负山、适于僧侣宦民坐禅礼佛的自然生态环境。

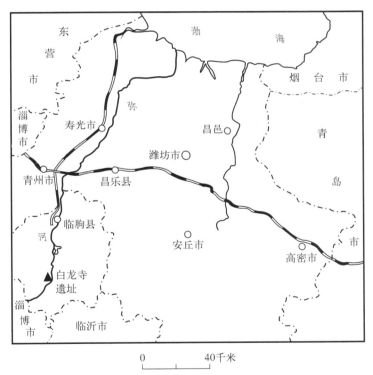

图一（fig.1） 临朐白龙寺地理位置示意图

一 地理环境

临朐县地处山东省的中部，面积1834平方千米。北与青州为邻，南与沂水、沂源接壤，西靠淄博，东与昌乐、安丘毗连（图二）。境内地势中南部为丘陵山区，北部地势较为平缓，境

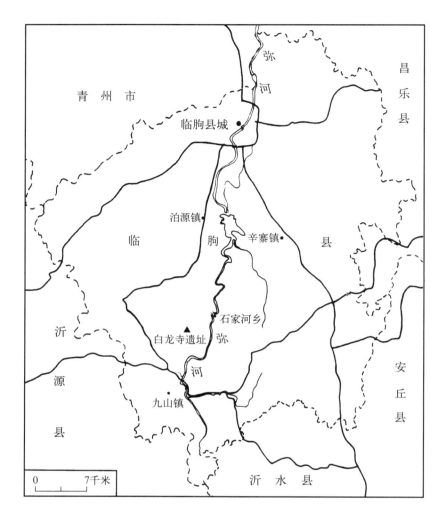

图二（fig.2）　白龙寺遗址位置示意图

内山地、丘陵占总面积的87%以上。这里为沂山隆起区，东接郯庐深大断裂带，北连昌乐凹陷，西跨五井断裂，因而具有隆起、凹陷、深大断裂三个级构造单元和断裂、褶皱等构造形态。出露地层主要有太古界泰山群，元古界震旦系，古生界寒武系、奥陶系、石炭系，中生界侏罗系、白垩系，新生界第三系、第四系。地势南高北低，南、西、东为低山、丘陵，中、北为平原，形成了三大地貌。低山中等侵蚀区和剥蚀堆积区，分布在县境内南部的大关、九山、蒋峪、石家河、寺头、五井及中南部冶源一带。低山丘陵侵蚀堆积区，其主要分布区域在县境内东部的上林、龙岗、七贤、柳山及东南部的大关、蒋峪、辛寨等乡镇。山前平原堆积区，多分布于县境内北部的城关、纸坊、杨善、七贤、龙岗、营子、冶源及东南部的蒋峪、辛寨等乡镇的部分地区。

　　临朐处于山东半岛水系，经流境内的河流主要是短源山溪性弥河、汶河及其支流。弥河古称巨洋河，发源于临朐沂山西麓天齐湾，顺坡蜿蜒西流，至临朐九山附近折向东北流，经过冶源水库，又经青州，于寿光广陵乡南半截河村，分三股入渤海。弥河的上、中游主要在临朐境内。

　　气候属鲁中南山地半湿润温和气候，年平均气温在12℃～13℃，1月份平均气温在-3℃，7月份的平均气温在25℃～26℃；年总日照时数在2400～2600小时，年平均日照率为58%；年降雨量在700～900毫米；降水量季节差别颇大，夏秋偏多，冬春较少。这里处在东亚季风区，风情季节变化明显，春季以南、东南、西南风为主，冬季以北、西北、东北风为主，夏、秋两季则以南风为主，年平均风速为2.6米／秒。

小时家庄佛寺建筑遗址位于山东省潍坊市临朐县石家河乡（现已并入寺头镇）小时家庄村西北，大时家庄村东山前台地上，北距临朐县城约30千米。坐标为北纬36°15′15.5″、东经118°28′05.1″，海拔258米。从石家河沿弥河西岸道路出发，行至大崮东村沿弥河支流右岸小路西行，到小时家庄村北上转弯后，山谷豁然开阔。此处四周环山，南侧开阔，相对隐蔽。遗址东西两侧有山洪冲沟，利于山洪排泄。遗址前有小河蜿蜒流淌向东流入弥河。四周山体足以阻挡冬季的寒风，夏季时可从山谷东南缺口进风，光照充足，冬暖夏凉，周围土地肥沃。从地理位置、自然环境来看，非常适宜人们居住，也是佛家建立佛教寺院的良好地点（图二；彩版一，1、2）。

二 历史沿革

据民国《临朐续志》卷六《沿革》载：临朐在唐尧时期传说为"丹朱之虚"。在商代称为"逄"。春秋时期称为"郱"。战国时期为齐国的骈邑，也曾称为"东阳"、"穆陵"。西汉属齐郡，称为"临朐"，后属琅琊郡，称为"朱虚"、"缾"、"临原"、"梧成"、"挍"、"城阳"。东汉属青州齐国，称"临朐"，王莽时期改为"监朐"，后属青州北海国，称"朱虚"。曹魏时期属城阳郡，也称"朱虚"，后称为"临朐"。晋朝属高密国，称为"临朐"，后属平昌郡，称为"朱虚"。刘宋时期属齐郡，前后分别称为"昌国"、"盘阳"、"西安"、"安平"，后属平昌郡，称为"朱虚"。元魏时期属胶州郡，称为"朱虚"。北齐时期属琅琊郡，称为"昌国"。北周时期也称为"昌国"。到隋代属北海郡，称为"临朐"。唐同属北海郡，称为"临朐"。五代、宋时期属青州，称为"临朐"。金代属益都路，称为"临朐"，"穆陵"。元代属益都路，称为"临朐"。明清时期属青州府，称为"临朐"。民国初，属胶东道，1925年改属淄青道，1927年直属山东省。中华人民共和国成立后，临朐属昌潍专区，1967年昌潍专区改称昌潍地区，1981年更名潍坊地区，1983年改称潍坊市，临朐顺次属之。

第二章 发掘整理

1999年4月，临朐县石家河乡弥河西岸，小时家庄村陆续发现大量石造像，有的造像还有题记，引起了省、市、县文物主管部门的重视。1999年8月，山东省文物考古研究所派李振光和胡常春对该遗址进行了调查和勘探，确认是一处北朝时期的佛教寺院遗址（图三）。

2001年，中国青州龙兴寺佛教窖藏造像大展在瑞士苏黎世、德国柏林、英国伦敦和美国华盛顿巡展，引起了世界史学界、考古界和美术界的广泛关注。主办单位瑞士苏黎世RIETBERG博物馆邀请苏黎世大学倪克鲁先生编辑出版展览图录。展览结束后，瑞士和列支敦士登国外考古学研究基金会指派倪克鲁先生到中国青州、诸城和临朐等地博物馆考察。

2002年8月，瑞士苏黎世大学倪克鲁先生到临朐博物馆考察北朝时期的佛造像，看到小时家庄遗址出土的佛造像，十分感兴趣。随后在临朐县博物馆副馆长宫德杰的陪同下到遗址现场进行考察。小时家庄位于弥河上游山谷之中，景色秀丽，流水潺潺，是修建佛教寺院的理想之地。倪克鲁先生出于对中国佛教艺术的挚爱，在脑海中勾画了一个对小时家庄佛教寺院遗址进行全面调查和深入研究的计划。

2003年2月，山东省文物考古研究所佟佩华、张振国、李振光到临朐小时家庄佛教遗址进行了考察，以获取更多的第一手资料，为向国家文物局申报中、瑞合作发掘临朐小时家庄佛教遗址项目做资料和业务技术准备。

2003年8月，国家文物局批复，同意瑞士苏黎世大学考古学者参观临朐白龙寺遗址发掘工地。2004年4月，中国政府批准了中、瑞合作发掘临朐白龙寺遗址项目。

2003年9月17日～10月30日，对临朐小时家庄遗址进行了第一次调查、勘探和发掘（图四）。主要有两项：一是在1999年8月调查勘探的基础上，对该遗址所在山前坡地进行了拉网式调查和大面积的勘探，进一步了解寺院遗址周围地区是否还存有其他古代遗存，以及寺院遗址文化堆积情况，为分析和认识小时家庄佛教遗址性质提供更充分的地下资料。二对小时家庄佛教遗址进行局部解剖，以印证1999年勘探的准确性，为下一步大面积发掘做准备。为此，组织两个组，一组进行考古调查和勘探，一组开挖两条探沟和一个探方，发掘面积约为160平方米。参加人员：中方有佟佩华（队长）、李振光（副队长）、吴双成和宫德杰；瑞方有布伦克（瑞方项目负责人）、倪克鲁（副队长）、孟为乐、贝昱瑞和温克（彩版二，1）。

2004年8月6日～10月9日，对临朐小时家庄遗址进行第二次勘探和发掘。本次工作主要有三项，一是在2003年第一次解剖性发掘的基础上，对小时家庄佛教遗址主要基址进行了全面清

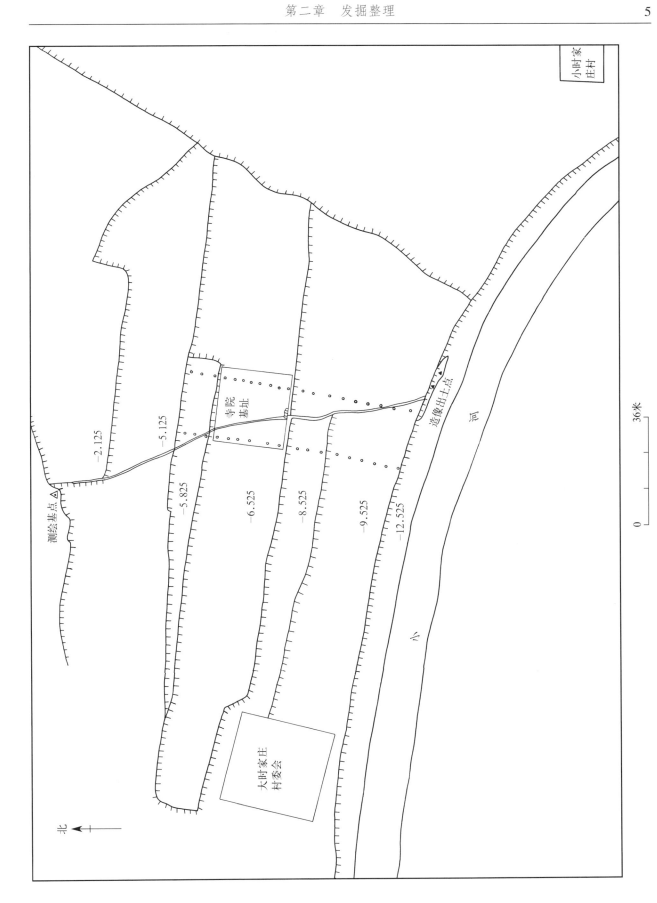

图三 (fig.3) 白龙寺遗址1999年考古勘探图

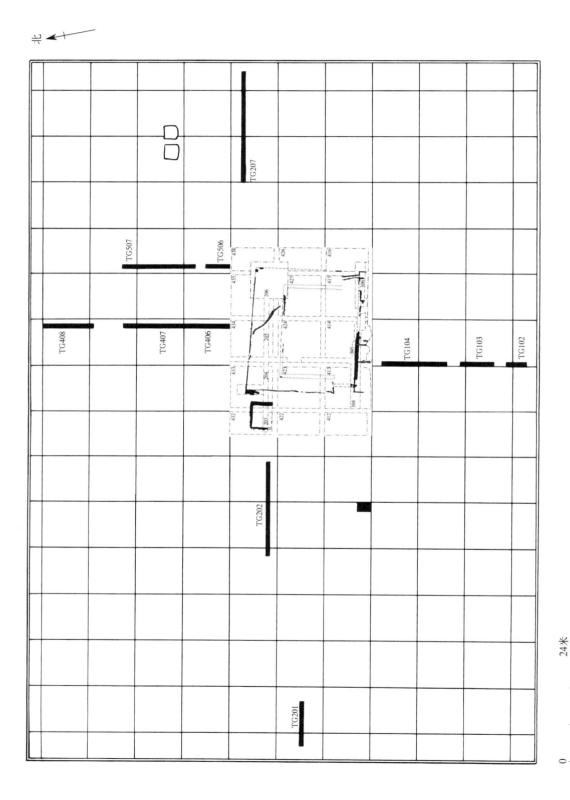

图四（fig.4） 白龙寺遗址发掘区示意图

理和发掘（彩版三，1），以了解该基础的平面布局、建筑结构和保存状况，获取更多的佛教造像、陶器、瓷器和铁器标本。二是在遗址的北、东、西三面，开挖七条探沟，了解其地层堆积以及是否还存在其他佛教遗迹。三是在佛教基址东北发掘两座烧制青砖的砖窑，以确定该寺院用砖是否为就地烧制。第二次发掘面积约1060平方米。参加人员：中方有佟佩华、李振光、吴双成和宫德杰；瑞方有布伦克（Helmut H. Brinker）、倪克鲁（Lukas Nickel）、孟为乐（Christian Muntwyler）、贝昱瑞（Jorrit A.M.Britschgi）和毕亚特（Beat Zollinger）（彩版二，2），还有：苏黎世大学的四个学生：苏玲（Sue-ling Gremli-Huber）、桑贺（Thanh Truong）、米歇尔（Michele Grieder）、石海玲（Geraldine Ramphal）。

2005年5月18日～26日，应瑞士苏黎世大学东亚美术史系的邀请，中国山东省文物考古研究所李传荣（项目中方负责人）、佟佩华、李振光和吴双成等人到瑞士苏黎世大学，就临朐小时家庄佛教遗址发掘资料整理和报告编写等问题进行交流和协商。瑞士苏黎世大学东亚美术史系主任布伦克、倪克鲁、贝昱瑞、孟为乐和毕亚特等参加了座谈。座谈中，中方介绍了发掘结束半年来资料整理的基本情况，提出了需要进一步交流和沟通的问题。瑞方介绍了发掘图纸整理的情况，就田野发掘中的问题发表了意见。经过友好、坦诚的协商，双方在许多问题上达成了共识。经双方努力，形成了发掘报告编写提纲，并确定了各章节中、瑞双方人员的分工。

2006年3月28日～4月8日，应中国山东省文物考古研究所邀请，瑞士苏黎世大学东亚美术史系倪克鲁、贝昱瑞等人到中国山东省文物考古研究所临淄工作站（彩版四，1），对临朐小时家庄佛教遗址发掘资料进行了基础性整理，并就许多问题进行了深入的讨论。中国山东省文物考古研究所佟佩华、李振光、吴双成和临朐县博物馆宫德杰等人参加了整理工作。中、瑞双方对出土陶器、瓷器和铁器等进行了清理、拼对、排比，并进行了摄影和记录。还到临朐博物馆对该馆历年来收集的小时家庄佛造像进行了拍照和记录。在临淄期间，双方还就报告的开本、双方文字对译、报告名称和署名等问题进行了讨论，基本上达成共识。

2009年9月19日～26日，中国山东省文物考古研究所佟佩华、李振光和吴双成在临淄工作站继续对出土文物进行挑选、排比和记录。

2010年8月17日～9月8日，应中国山东省文物考古研究所邀请，已转到英国伦敦大学任职的倪克鲁先生到中国山东省文物考古研究所临淄工作站，对临朐小时家庄佛教遗址发掘报告进行共同编写工作。中国山东省文物考古研究所佟佩华、李振光、吴双成和宫德杰等人参加了编写工作。双方共同完成了初稿撰写、线图绘制、照片挑选等工作。倪克鲁先生完成了报告文稿提要的撰写工作。双方还就报告的出版事宜交换了意见。

2014年10月13～21日，中国山东省文物考古研究所佟佩华、李振光、吴双成与英国伦敦大学倪克鲁在济南完成了报告初稿。倪克鲁先生依据报告初稿完成了英文的翻译工作。在英文稿的翻译工作中，英国伦敦大学亚非学院博士研究生吴虹、欧阳碧晴、林郡仪给予了很大帮助（彩版四，2）。

2015年8月27～31日，中国山东省文物考古研究所佟佩华、李振光与英国伦敦大学倪克鲁在济南完成了报告中文稿和英文稿的校订工作。

　　小时家庄佛教建筑遗址在发掘之初，定名为"白龙寺遗址"。据明嘉靖三十一年（公元1552年）《嘉靖临朐县志》载"县南65里有白龙寺一座"；清康熙十一年（公元1672年）《康熙临朐县志》载"白龙寺，即十字院，在常庄社，至县60里"。县志中记载的地理位置和小时家庄佛教建筑遗址位置相近，且遗址周围百姓非常信仰白龙，在遗址北禅堂崮一带有"白龙神庙"的刻铭，东北方的白龙洞亦有白龙神庙的建筑基址残碑断碣，有一保存完整的皇帝敕建白龙神庙的御碑，附近还有仙姑庙、泰山行宫遗址及碑刻等佛教遗存。因此在发掘之初，将遗址定名为"白龙寺遗址"。在遗址实际发掘工作中，没有发现相关的文字证据，依照考古学遗址常规命名的方法，应该命名为"小时家庄佛寺建筑遗址"，但考虑到在发掘之前及发掘过程中已经使用，仍然沿用"白龙寺遗址"的名称。

　　本书报告了中国和瑞士联合考古队，2003年和2004年对中国山东临朐小时家庄"白龙寺"佛教遗址进行调查、勘探和发掘的成果。书中注意用照片、线图、拓片等多种方式，图文并茂地展示了遗迹及出土遗物，给关心和研究北朝时期佛教考古的学者提供了更加直观的科学资料；介绍了我们源于第一手资料所得到的认识，以及相关问题的思考，有些问题我们也觉得还很难说清楚，希望得到学术界的批评和指导；分析了中、瑞双方考古理论、考古手段和考古方法的异同，初步总结了我们通过交流和沟通，基本达成一致并经过实践检验的工作方法，希望能够引起讨论。

第三章 工作方法

考古学诞生于19世纪初的西方，考古学的两大支柱地层学和类型学，分别来自于地质学的地层学和生物学的分类学。20世纪初，近代考古学传入中国，并很快在中国生根、开花、结果。

遵循考古学基本理论地层学和类型学是一致的，由于考古学在西方和中国的发展时间和阶段不同、科学技术发展水平不同、生产生活方式不同、思想文化观念不同，因而在发掘手段和工作方法上也会有所不同。在我们开始商谈合作发掘项目时，双方都已经意识到如何充分交流、深入了解、相互沟通、取长补短、达成共识就成为合作成功与否的关键所在。由于中、瑞双方都对这个问题有一个基本的、清醒的认识，所以我们在立项过程中、考古发掘之前、考古发掘之中、发掘结束之后，一直到资料整理和报告编写时，都在不断地就考古学的理论、方法和技术等问题进行交流和切磋（彩版三，2）。我们遵循考古学的基本原理，考古发掘中，按照文化堆积从下到上积累形成，逆向顺序从上至下一层一层揭露，遇有重要遗迹先行发掘二分之一或者三分之一。在资料整理过程中，将遗迹和遗物分类别和形制进行梳理，参照地层学提供的先后顺序，排列出演进规律，划段分期给予归纳总结。当然也有一方难以说服一方，问题暂时搁置的时候。总体来讲，相互沟通比较顺利，也成为我们圆满完成合作发掘的保证。

在合作发掘过程中，我们先后运用了考古调查、考古勘探和考古发掘等基本手段，以揭示小时家庄佛教遗址的历史面目。考古调查工作主要是发掘之初，我们的调查没有局限于1999年调查勘探确定的范围之内，而是扩大到整个台地以至于山顶。调查也包括向村民特别是七、八十岁的老人询访，也包括暴雨过后到山坡、河旁、沟边捡拾有可能新暴露的遗物。在寻访中，我们的诚挚，特别是瑞士学者不远万里来到深山峡谷保护文物的行动，感动了不少村民。许多村民捐献了保存多年的佛教遗物。按照中国政府的规定，我们上报县文物主管部门给予精神奖励和物质奖励。以洛阳铲为标志的中国考古勘探，为瑞方学者所称赞，我们用普探结合重点勘探的方法，搞清了整个台地的文化堆积情况，确定了寺院遗址的范围，排除了存在其他佛教遗存的可能性。

一 考古发掘

考古发掘分两个阶段进行。

　　第一阶段：2003年在寺院遗址上开挖了十字形解剖探沟，以确定寺院遗址的文化堆积、建筑范围和保存状况，见有砖瓦或重要遗迹立即停止下挖，测图、照相和记录后回填，待下一阶段全面揭露后统一处理。

　　第二阶段：2004年对寺院遗址进行了全面发掘，共开挖10米×10米探方9个和探沟7条，清理建筑基址1套、砖窑2座。通过发掘，基本上掌握了寺院遗址的基本内涵（彩版三，1）。

　　在商谈和制定发掘方案时，我们遇到的第一个问题就是布置探方方法问题。按照中国目前通行的发掘布方是：正方向，一象限，5米×5米探方，预留北隔梁和东隔梁，以有效的控制地层。当前瑞士以至于欧洲采取全面揭露的方法，以有利于直观展现同一时期遗存的整体性和客观性。在这个问题上，一开始中、瑞双方学者争执不休，谁也说不服谁。后来鉴于中方学者和技工都没有全面揭露的实践和经验，为了保险起见，双方都做了部分妥协。最后确定发掘方法：在遗址西南方向合适位置设立固定总基点，一象限网格覆盖整个寺院遗址，采用10米×10米的大探方，预留的隔梁遇有跨方的遗迹，做好资料后随时打掉。探方的布置依地形采用自然方向，南北向隔梁北偏东11°。在发掘的实际过程中，双方都感觉到这个方法还是可行的，整个发掘过程也因此得以顺利进行。

　　在商谈和制定发掘方案时，我们遇到的第二个问题就是所发现的文化层和文化遗迹的编号问题。中国目前普遍流行的编号方法是将文化层和灰坑、灰沟、房址、墓葬、水井等遗迹分类。用加圈的阿拉伯数字表示文化层，用H表示灰坑，用G表示灰沟，用F表示房址，用M表示墓葬，用J表示水井等等，并按照发现的早晚用阿拉伯数字依次排序冠名。而瑞士以及欧洲采用将文化层和灰坑、灰沟、房址、墓葬、水井等遗迹以暴露早晚统一编排一个顺序号，以表示发掘的客观性。发掘结束进行资料整理时，再分析推测其用途。在双方交流和沟通中，中国学者接受了瑞士专家的做法，在小时家庄佛教遗址发掘中对文化层和遗迹统一编号。统一编号的顺序是按照文化层和遗迹发现早晚排序的，并不表示文化层和遗迹本身叠压和打破的早晚关系。在发掘的实际过程中，中国学者并没有感到什么不便，只是改变人的惯性思维和例行做法需要一定的时间，或更多次的重复实践。

　　在合作发掘过程中，我们还先后对发掘中发现遗迹和遗物的记录方式进行了交流和沟通，形成许多共识。瑞士学者专门从欧洲带来了电子全站仪（彩版五，1），我们以遗址对面山坡上一个蓄水池的一角做为我们发掘区的固定基点（彩版五，2），用一个象限1米间距方格网覆盖整个遗址区域。在发掘区东北角设立全站仪的固定基点（彩版六，1），准确标明基站的高程、经度、纬度。在发掘区四周用标识牌标示方格网的地面位置（彩版六，2），以便于将某一文化堆积或遗迹准确地套合到发掘区方格网总图中。在发掘实际过程中，我们感觉到电子全站仪提高了绘图精度，测量高程可以复原某一个文化层和遗迹的立体结构，特别是发掘佛教寺院这样的大型遗迹，可以确定其前后、左右相对高程，为分析遗迹性质和用途提供了准确数据。

二 绘图

瑞士学者用加厚的硫酸纸印制了白龙寺遗址专用图纸。图纸右上方用中、英和德文印有遗址的名称和发掘单位，图例部分提示逐一填写比例、绘图员、日期、位置、堆积号码和图号，规范明确。图纸为标准A3尺寸（420毫米×297毫米）。图纸上在50毫米网格交叉点上标有"＋"，我们采用1∶20的比例，每个"＋"字交叉点间距离为100厘米。我们还对发现最多的砖涂以天蓝色，瓦片涂以浅黄色，一目了然。用加厚的硫酸纸绘图还便于将所绘的平、剖面图数字化，供资料整理中图纸的拼接和出版制作。绘图的比例，根据发掘对象的大小，我们还绘制了1∶50和1∶100两种比例尺的图纸（彩版七～一〇）。

三 摄影

瑞士专家带来了2004年当时最好的尼康D1数码照相机。我们对所有文化层和遗迹的平、剖面图进行了全方位的拍摄。对于较长的探沟剖面和寺院的墙体，我们按照相机能跨越的最大相幅，分段做标记逐一拍摄，以利于在电脑中整体拼接。本报告公布的探沟剖面图和寺院墙体长幅照片就是这样完成的。在拍摄时，我们还放置指北针、米尺和标牌。放置指北针有利于人们对该堆积方位的判断。放置米尺有利于人们对该堆积体量的感受。放置的标牌为活插式，注明遗址的字母缩写代码、发掘年度和堆积编号，有利于室内整理时照片的清点，与文化层和遗迹的对照（彩版一一，1、2，一二，1）。

四 文字记录

我们采用填写"发掘记录表"方式，以10米×10米大探方为基本单位，每一个文化层或遗迹，填写一张。记录表包括基本情况、层位关系、深度厚度、堆积描述、形状描述、遗物采集、测试标本采集位置、草图、备注（发掘经过及其他）共九大部分。细数一个堆积单位要填写五十多个要素点，可谓详之又详。在层位关系栏中，明确列有打破、叠压两种关系。提示发掘者首先搞清楚该堆积单位与其相关单位的基本关系。在堆积描述中列有土色、土质、致密度、堆积形状、包含物、保存状况、清理方式、堆积性质和其他九项，其内容有的由发掘者选择，有的由发掘者填写。基本规范型制和描述，有利于资料整理时的统一，避免同一个形态几种不同描述情况出现。测试标本采集栏中，提示有C14、孢粉/植硅石、浮选土样和其他，也体现目前考古发掘和研究的新导向。我们还设有"小件登记表"，以探方为单位，登记出土文物，以便于资料整理清点和记录。这些规范的答题式记录卡方式，也方便了资料整理阶段输入电脑。

　　最后说明的是，瑞士学者带来的发掘手铲为长条形平头式，与中国山东通用的手铲相似，我们用起来非常顺手（彩版一二，2）。

第四章　文化堆积

一　TG201北壁剖面

探沟分布于东西向967～977米处，东西长10.00、南北宽1.00米，北壁剖面位于南北向425米处（图五）。

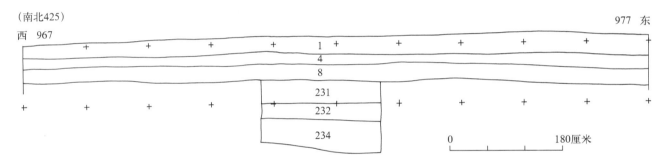

图五（fig.5）　TG201北壁剖面图

堆积1，现代耕土层。堆积厚0.24～0.52米。较疏松的褐色粉沙土，含植物根系、烧土颗粒。内出少量灰陶片、白瓷片、青花瓷片。分布全工地。

堆积4，黄褐沙土层。距地表深0.24～0.52、厚0.12～0.24米。较为疏松。堆积较为平整。内出有灰陶片、烧土。

堆积8，浅灰褐色粉沙土层。距地表深0.32～0.56、厚0.22～0.34米。土质较致密，由北向南倾斜。分布在建筑址所在的第二台地上。

堆积231，黄褐色粉沙土层。距地表深0.70、厚0.30米。呈斜坡状堆积。出有陶片、瓷片，应为宋代堆积层。

堆积232，黄褐色黏土层。距地表深1.12、厚0.28米。内中出有少量瓷片、烧土、炭屑。应为宋代堆积层。

堆积234，黄褐色粉沙土层。距地表深1.32、厚0.53米。土质较为疏松。

以下是生土层，黑色黏土。

二　TG202北壁剖面

探沟分布于东西向1008.5～1029米，东西长20.50、南北宽1.00米，北壁分布在南北向432.4米（图六）。

堆积1，耕土层。堆积1下分布有堆积216、217。堆积217为大的灰坑状堆积，在坑的东部近壁处，存在大量石块，为晚期灰坑。堆积216为南北向晚期灰沟，分布在东西向1024米处，内有较多的石块。

堆积4，同前。

堆积213，为黄褐色沙土堆积，为水淤积形成。距地表深0.36、厚0～0.52米。呈坡状堆积分布。其下为堆积6。分布在探沟向东至T432。

堆积214、215，为南北向口宽底窄的浅沟，东西宽0.78、深0.30米。堆积214为215的沟内堆积，为较疏松的黄褐色沙土，内含碎瓦、瓷片以及较多的小石块、烧土颗粒、淤沙。

以下是生土层。

三　T432～T436南壁剖面

南北向430米东西长剖面。分布于南北向430、东西1035～1075米处，剖面长40.00米（图七）。

堆积1，耕土层。分布于整个遗址。

堆积19，较致密浅灰褐粉沙土。距地表深0.20～0.35、堆积厚0.30米。分布于发掘区的东部。

堆积20，较致密浅黄褐色黏土，含粗沙颗粒。距地表深0.12～0.41、厚0～0.33米。堆积由北向南倾斜。分布在发掘区的东部。

堆积21，较致密黄褐色粉沙黏土。距地表深0.11～0.64、厚0～0.23米。出有铁器残片。由西向东倾斜堆积。分布于发掘区的东部。

堆积63，较致密黄褐色粗沙亚黏土。距地表深0.12～0.70、厚0～0.30米。分布于发掘区的东半部。

堆积44、44A，较致密浅灰褐色粉沙土。距地表深0.65～0.70、厚0～0.17米。含烧土、草木灰，堆积由北向南倾斜，分布于发掘区的东部。

堆积19、20、21、63、44、44A，分布于堆积1下，堆积4上。应为因大水冲刷在遗址东半部形成大的洼地，短时期内形成的洼地堆积。在1058～1059米处分布一道呈弧状分布的石头遗迹（堆积22）。

堆积4，黄褐色粉沙土。距地表深0.11～0.18、厚0～0.35米。内含陶片、烧土块。堆积呈水平状，分布于发掘区的西半部。

堆积5，较致密的灰褐色粉沙土。距地表深0.42、厚0～0.13米。堆积由北向南倾斜，分布于发掘区的中北部。

堆积68，疏松黑灰色粉沙土。距地表深0.30～0.54、厚0～0.28米。内含少量瓷片。堆积由北向南倾斜，分布于发掘区中部。

堆积117，较致密黄褐色细沙土。距地表深0.45～0.71、厚0～0.17米。内含陶片、瓷片、少量石块、烧土。应为淤积而成水平状堆积

堆积118，灰褐色沙土。距地表深0.64、厚0～0.12米。包含较多陶片、瓷片以及少许石块、烧土颗粒。应为水冲积而成的水平状堆积。

堆积163，较致密黄褐色细沙土、淤沙土。距地表深0.55、厚0～0.12米。内含少量陶片、石块。水淤积形成的水平状堆积，分布于发掘区的中部。

堆积69，较致密的浅灰褐土粉沙土，含少量烧土颗粒、炭屑。距地表深0.50～0.82、厚0～0.24米。堆积由北向南倾斜，分布于发掘区的中西部。

堆积195，较致密黄褐色粉沙土。距地表深0.75～1.05、厚0～0.24米。包含砖、瓦、石块大量白石灰，应为南侧台基上瓦顶建筑倒塌堆积。坡状堆积，分布于中心台基北侧。

堆积70，较致密灰褐色粉沙土。距地表深0.08～1.12、厚0～0.36米。含烧土、草木灰、碳颗粒，出有大量陶片、瓦当、瓷片。该层堆积由北向南倾斜，为北侧建筑倒塌倾斜下来的堆积，分布在台基的北侧、西侧下陷庭院部分。

堆积64，疏松的灰褐土，内含炭灰、烧土颗粒。距地表深0.97～1.30、厚0～0.35米。内含大量陶片、瓷片、瓦片。堆积由北向南倾斜，应为房屋废弃后的堆积。

堆积223，为台基北侧下陷庭院的地面。距地表深0.11～0.18、厚0～0.35米。台基的北侧部分用卵石铺垫。地面比较平整，南侧略低，利于水流排泄。

西侧小房子内的堆积有：堆积6、7、29。

堆积6，较为致密的浅黄褐色粉沙土，内包含粗沙、零星碳屑。距地表深0.18～1.30、厚0.13～0.18米。分布在发掘区的西部，叠压在残存墙体之上。

堆积7，较致密的黄褐色粉砂亚黏土，含烧土颗粒、零星碳屑。距地表深0.39～0.42、厚0.12～0.24米。分布在小房子内，呈水平状分布。为房子废弃堆积。

堆积29，为小房子内的活动地面，土质经踩踏较为坚硬，可以分许多薄层，表面光亮。厚0.13米。

四　TG207北壁剖面

探沟分布在东西1090～1114米处，长24.00、南北宽1.00米，剖面分布在南北向438米处（图八）。

探沟内文化堆积较为简单，分布较为平整。

从上到下有堆积1、19、228、229、20、230、21，探沟的中部地势略低，与西侧发掘区内文化堆积相对应，皆为晚期文化堆积。探沟内没有发现与建筑址相关的遗迹。

五　TG408东壁剖面

探沟分布于南北向469～480米，长11.00、东西宽1.00米，东壁剖面位于东西向1059米处（图九）。

沟内堆积分为七层，为沙土和淤沙土，土质比较单纯，堆积比较平整，为山洪冲积形成的自然堆积。

六　TG407东壁剖面

探沟分布于南北向440～456米，南北长16.00、东西宽1.00米，东壁剖面分布于东西向1059米处（图一〇）。

探沟内的堆积有堆积1、19、20、21、63、71、72。

堆积1、19、20、21，同前述。

堆积63，较致密黄褐色细沙土、淤沙土。距地表深0.5～0.66、厚0～0.14米。内含少许陶片、石块，应为山洪冲积形成。

堆积72，为东西向长沟。敞口，斜壁，口宽9.06、沟深1.70米。

堆积71，为沟内堆积，分为12层，多淤沙、石子，不见陶片、瓷片。

七　T414、424、434西壁剖面

分布在东西1050、南北向412～444.5米处，剖面长32.50米（图一一；彩版一三）。

东西1050米，南北长剖面与TG407、408、104、103、102相结合，反映了遗址南北的堆积情况。

堆积1，现代耕土层。堆积厚0.12～0.28米。分布在发掘区的全部。

堆积4A，较疏松的黄褐色粉沙土。距地表深0.11～0.30、厚0～0.30米。内中出有陶片、瓷片、烧土块。分布在中部台地及北侧台地的南部。

堆积4B，致密的黄褐色沙土。距地表深0.43～0.60、厚0～0.30米。分布在发掘区中部台地的南半部。

堆积5，较疏松的灰褐色粉沙土。距地表深0.18～0.42、厚0～0.23米。内中出有大量的瓷片、陶片及少量的瓦当。分布在发掘区中部台地的北半部。

堆积23，紧密的黄褐色粗沙淤土。距地表深0.12～0.59、厚0～0.40米。分布在发掘区的北侧

台地上。

堆积24，细密黄褐色黏土。距地表深0.50～0.60、厚0～0.30米。分布在发掘区的北侧台地上。

堆积71和堆积72在TG407和TG408内介绍。

堆积68，疏松黑灰色粉沙土。距地表深0.30～0.54、厚0～0.28米。内含少量瓷片。堆积由北向南倾斜，分布于发掘区中部。

堆积117，较致密黄褐色细沙土。距地表深0.45、厚0～0.10米。内含少量陶片、石块、烧土颗粒，应为水淤积而成。

堆积118，灰褐色沙土。距地表深0.47、厚0～0.09米。内含较多陶片、少许石块、少许烧土颗粒，应为水冲积而成。

堆积163，较致密黄褐色细沙土。距地表深0.55、厚0～0.12米。内含少许陶片、石块，应为水淤积形成。

堆积69，较致密的浅灰褐粉沙土，含少量烧土颗粒、炭屑。距地表深0.50～0.82、厚0～0.24米。堆积分布在发掘区的中西部，由北向南倾斜。

堆积195，较致密黄褐色粉沙土。距地表深0.75～1.05、厚0～0.24米。包含砖、瓦、石块大量白石灰，应为南侧台基上瓦顶建筑倒塌堆积。坡状堆积，分布于中心台基北侧。

堆积70，较致密灰褐色粉沙土，含烧土、草木灰、碳颗粒。距地表深0.70、厚0.12～0.52米。出有大量瓦片、瓦当、瓷片，该层堆积分布在台基的北侧西侧下陷庭院部分，堆积由北向南倾斜，为北侧建筑倒塌倾斜下来的垃圾堆积。

堆积64，疏松的灰褐土，内含炭灰、烧土颗粒。距地表深0.90～1.10、厚0.15～0.48米。内含大量陶片、瓷片、瓦片。堆积由北向南倾斜，应为房屋废弃后的堆积。

堆积218，灰褐色粉沙土。距地表深1.10、厚0～0.18米。内含少量陶片、石块、炭屑，为垃圾土。分布在中心台基北侧庭院的北部。

堆积219和堆积243为中心台基北侧庭院内的坑状堆积。

堆积209，浅黄褐粉沙土。距地表深0.50～0.70、厚0～0.20米。内含少许周代陶片、石块，为台基垫土。分布在中心台基上。

堆积210，黄褐色粉沙土。在解剖探沟内发现，为坑状堆积，未见遗物。

堆积240，黄褐色粉沙土。距地表深0.50～0.85、厚0～0.35米。内含少量周代陶片，为台基垫土。

堆积241，为周代灰坑。

堆积242，为周代文化层堆积。

八　TG104西壁剖面

分布在东西1050、南北向396～408米处（图一二）。南北长13.00米。探沟内有堆积1、33、34、101、102、103、104、105、106、107。

堆积1，为耕土层。

堆积33，略松浅灰褐色沙土，内含陶片石子。为近代扰乱层。

堆积34，较疏松灰褐色沙土，内含陶片、瓷片。为近代文化层

堆积99、100，为口宽底窄的东西向灰沟，分布在堆积33下，为晚期灰沟。

堆积37、38，为较疏松黄褐色沙土，可能为灰沟或灰坑

堆积101、102、103、104、105、106，为周代灰沟内文化堆积。

堆积107，为敞口圜底的大沟。

九　TG103西壁剖面

分布在东西1050、南北向383～391米处（图一三）。南北长8.00米。沟内堆积简单，有堆积1、33、39、105。

堆积1、33，同TG104的堆积1、33。

堆积39，较疏松浅灰褐沙土。内含较多的泥质陶片，为宋代后文化层。

堆积105，同前。为周代文化堆积。

一〇　TG102西壁剖面

分布在东西1050、南北向376～381米处（图一四）。南北长5米。探沟内堆积有堆积1、33，同前。堆积33由北向南倾斜。

一一　公路北侧断崖剖面

共清理三段（图一五），西部、中间两段东西长1.00米，东部一段东西长6.00米。堆积有1、4、94、95、96、97、98。堆积1、4同北侧台上堆积。堆积94～98皆为从北侧台上倾倒下来的废弃堆积，内含较多的陶片、瓷片、建筑构件。下部为淤沙和石块，为河边堆积。

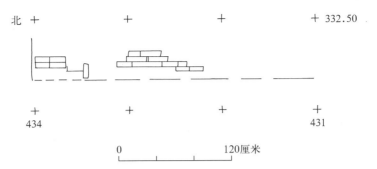

图二五（fig.25）　T436堆积65东侧高台砖墙前视图

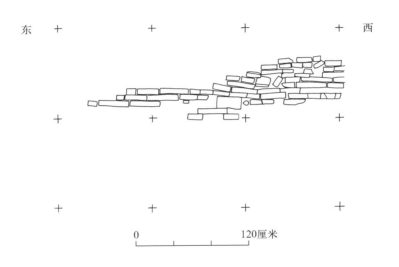

图二六（fig.26）　西侧内庭南侧砖墙前视图

6．长方形台基南侧的上下通道

建筑基址使用延续时间较长，上下台基的通道经过多次修建，从保存遗迹看，可能分为三期（图二七；彩版二六，1）。

早期通道

长方形台基的南侧东端仅存一道砖墙，分布在东西向1063.6米处。由台基的南侧砖墙向南砌筑南北向砖墙，残存南北0.80米，仅剩四层砖，上部向西倾斜。该道砖墙为台基使用时修筑的，应为早期开始修建台基时修建使用的上下通道的残留（彩版二六，2）。

中期通道

由砖石混筑的通道护坡墙堆积165、166及其内侧填土堆积组成。台基南侧中部分布堆积188，中部较高，向西倾斜。灰褐色粉沙土，土质较为紧密，土中包含物较少，含少量瓦片、石灰颗粒。厚0.50米。在堆积188上面垒砌两条南北向砖墙，破坏严重。

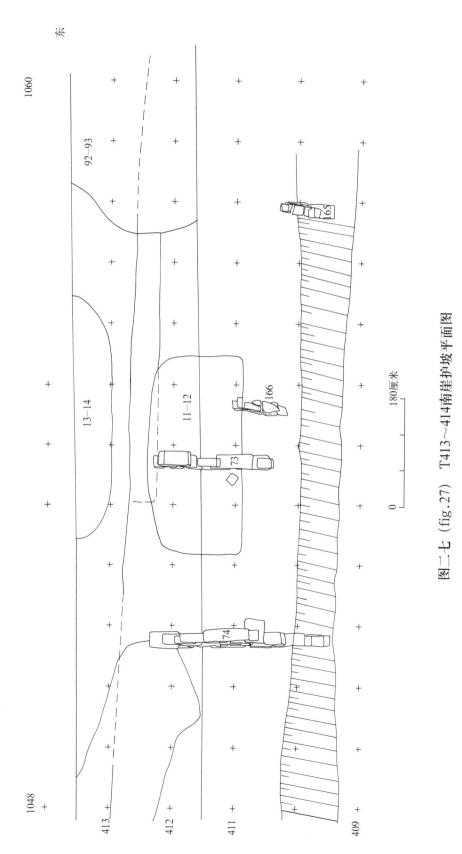

图二七（fig.27）　T413～414南崖护坡平面图

东侧砖墙堆积165，分布在东西向1058米处，底铺石头，上部南北向顺砌单砖墙体，墙体南北长0.88、残存高0.40米。砖墙向西侧倾斜（彩版二七，1）。

西侧砖墙堆积166，分布在东西向1054.6米处。底铺石头，上部南北向顺砌单砖墙体，砖墙上砌筑斜立板瓦，南北长0.90、残高0.30米。砖墙向东倾斜（彩版二七，2）。两道砖墙东西宽3.52米，两者皆向内侧倾斜，应为一组设施。砖墙与北侧台基对应，分布在台基的正中，可能为台基南侧上下台基通道的东西两面护坡。其内有堆积186和187，包含物较少，共同构成通道。其做法可能是用砖石砌筑两侧护坡，内侧用废弃物填满形成上下台基的通道。该期通道的使用应该在建筑使用一段时间并部分破坏以后。

晚期通道

石墙堆积74，分布在东西向1050.8米处（彩版二八，1）。用长条形石板垒砌而成，南北长2.90、残高1.06米。石墙上部向东倾斜。其东侧垫土较乱，内中包含大量的瓦片、陶片、瓷片、白灰土等，是用建筑废弃堆积填塞的。应为北部台上建筑废弃后建造的，是将堆积165和166间的通道向西加宽形成的，这时期通道东西宽7.20米。

石墙堆积73，分布在东西向1053.7米处（彩版二八，2），保存较长。底部铺石头，其上南北向长条形石板垒砌而成。长1.92、残高0.50米上部向东倾斜。是在晚于石墙74的堆积175、176内挖槽建造的，该道石墙应晚于西侧的石墙堆积74，其性质有待探讨。

二　小房子

位于建筑基址的西北角，东侧由高台与建筑群联通。

房子为东西长方形，内侧东西长5.04、南北宽4.32米。东西墙与北墙用土石夯筑而成，残存墙体东墙宽0.84～0.94、北墙宽0.60、墙体残高0.80米。南侧无墙，发现一块石头柱础，柱础中心距离西墙1.60米，可能为二立柱中的西侧立柱。地面平整，有踩踏形成的而活动地面，并发现大片火烧烤形成的红烧土面。房内残存大量瓦片，应为房子倒塌形成。根据残存迹象。复原房子的结构应为坐北向南夯土墙瓦顶建筑，南侧二立柱支撑顶部的瓦顶建筑。由房内发现的大片烧土面看，应为烧炊用房屋（图二八；彩版二九，1～3）。

三　陶窑

共2座。分布在遗址的东北角，建筑址的东北部。距离东侧高台砖墙27米。两座陶窑东西相距1.00米，为同时期烧造陶器或建筑构件的两座陶窑。借助北侧断崖，在生土中掏挖而成（图二九；彩版三〇、三一）。

1．堆积224

0　　　　　　120厘米

图二八（fig.28）　小房子平、剖面图

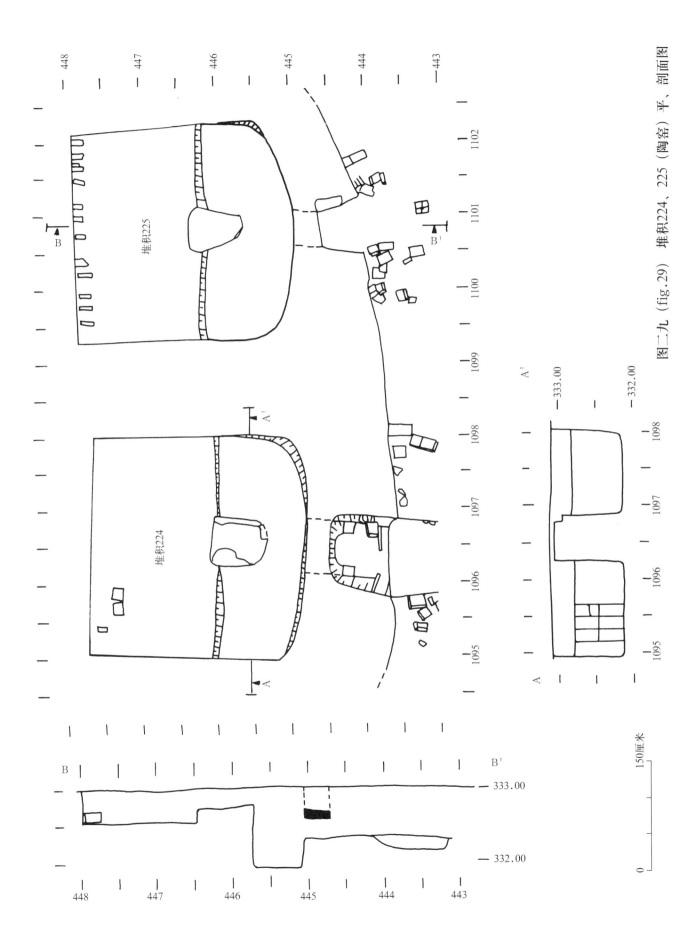

图二九（fig.29） 堆积224、225（陶窑） 平、剖面图

堆积225

堆积224

B

B'

A'

A'

A

A

333.00

332.00

B

B'

333.00

332.00

150厘米

0

443 444 445 446 447 448

443 444 445 446 447 448

1095 1096 1097 1098 1099 1100 1101 1102

为西侧陶窑。

窑门，南向，方向180°。窑门两侧用单砖顺砌砖墙，门宽0.46、高0.30米。火道进深0.40米，两侧被火烧烤成红色，烧烤面较厚。

工作间，窑门南面有长方形工作间，东西长0.82~1.16、南北进深0.90米。工作间南侧地势低十几厘米，与东侧陶窑工作间相连，地面分布大量的青砖。

窑室，平面为南侧略呈弧边的正方形。东西长3.02、南北宽2.88米，窑室壁残高0.4米。窑室四壁烧烤成青灰色烧烤面，厚12厘米。

火塘，位于窑室内南半部，南北长1.10米，较窑室台面下深0.46米。火塘的底部残存大量草木灰土。

分火柱，在火塘的北部中间紧贴窑室高台处有一立柱，立柱平面呈不规则长方形，南北长0.80、东西宽0.56~0.68米，立柱南侧呈圆弧形。立柱高0.90米，比北侧台面高出0.24米，顶部残。

器物台，位于窑室的北半部，为生土台，挖火塘时保留形成。台面平整光滑，火烧烤成青灰色，南北长1.70米。台的南侧立面用单砖平铺贴面，做台子的保护面，在分火柱的西侧还残留有台外贴砖。

在窑室的器物台上，残存青砖三块。

2. 堆积225

为东侧陶窑。位于堆积224东侧1.00米，两座陶窑东西平行分布，后壁分布在东西一线上。南侧活动地面相连，分布一层青砖。应与堆积224作为一组陶窑使用。

窑门，南向，方向180°。在生土中掏挖形成，呈宽扁圆角长方形，东西宽0.52、高0.26米。火道进深0.33米。两侧被火烧烤成红色，烧烤面较厚。

工作间，窑门南面有梯形工作间，东西宽0.48~0.80、南北进深1.00米。工作间南侧地势下低二、三十厘米，与西侧陶窑工作间相连，地面分布大量的青砖。

窑室，平面为南侧略呈弧边的正方形。东西宽2.84~3.00、南北长2.96米，窑室壁残高0.44米。窑室四壁烧烤成青灰色烧烤面，厚12厘米。

火塘，位于窑室内南半部，南北宽1.16米，较窑室台面下深0.62米。火塘的底部残存大量草木灰土。

分火柱，在火塘的北部中间紧贴窑室高台处有一立柱，立柱平面略呈梯形，南北长0.72、东西宽0.32~0.62米，南侧立柱面呈圆弧形。立柱高0.86米，比北侧台面高出0.18米，顶部残。

器物台，位于窑室的北半部，为生土台，挖火塘时保留形成。台面平整光滑，火烧烤成青灰色。

在窑室的器物台上，残存青砖一排，东西12块，砖之间间隔0.10~0.14米，南北成行排列。

四　其他遗迹

1. 烧灶

堆积122，位于T434内，开口在堆积5下。平面呈束腰弧边长条形。灶坑呈长椭圆形，周边被火烧烤形成烧土面，寰底，底部呈青灰色，多草木灰。残长1.10、深0.36米。灶门处放置一长条形石块。投柴间呈圆角长条形，长0.98、深0.08～0.16米。为烧炊用灶坑（图三〇；彩版三三）。

2. 灰坑

遗址发现的灰坑多为晚期扰乱形成。在房址使用时期建筑台面保存较好。在中心台基的北侧下陷部分，发现有灰坑。

堆积196～202，为灰坑及坑内堆积。堆积202为灰坑的壁和底，呈不规则形长方形，长3.88、宽2.42、深0.40～1.26米。内部堆积分为六层，内含大量的陶片、瓷片、瓦片、造像残块、白灰土、烧土颗粒。为人为挖坑堆积而成（图三一）。

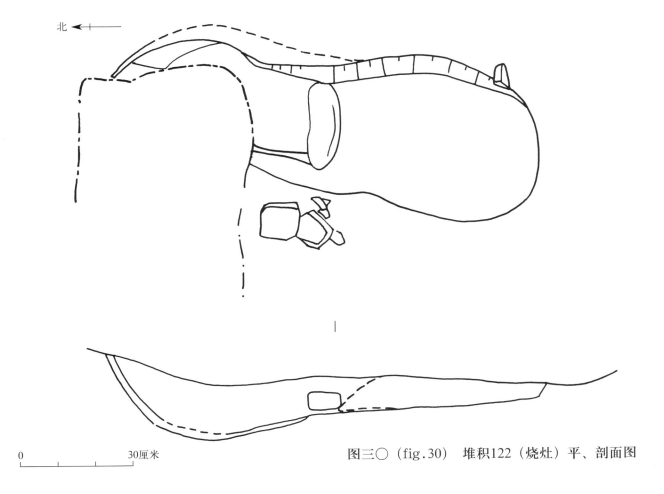

北 ←

0 ⊢——————⊣ 30厘米

图三〇（fig.30）　堆积122（烧灶）平、剖面图

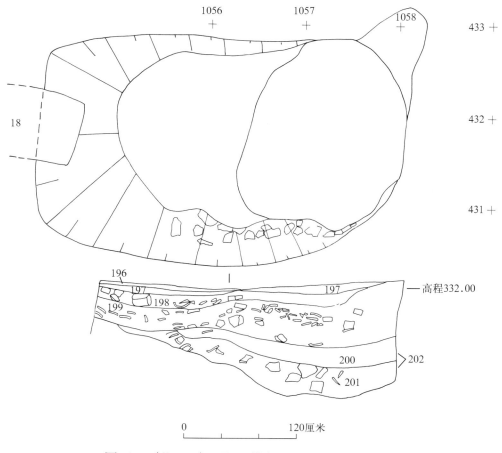

图三一（fig.31）　T434堆积196～202平、剖面图

3．灰沟

2条。

堆积99、100在TG104内发现，沟浅，局部进行清理。

堆积71、72，分布在发掘区的北部，建筑基址北侧高台的北侧。开口于堆积63下，沟口分布在南北向442.8～451.9米处。沟南北宽9.10米，为大敞口、斜壁圜底东西向深沟，深1.68米。沟内堆积十二层，堆积较纯，为黄褐色或灰褐色沙土、细沙或淤土，结构紧密。未见陶瓷片等遗物。经勘探，大沟西起小房子的北侧，西端较浅，向东直行，沿陶窑的西侧转向南行。

4．墓葬

发现墓葬1座。

堆积60～62，开口于堆积21下。长方形土坑竖穴，长2.01、宽1.15、深1.10米。用长条形石板和基础残砖垒砌成圆角长方形，墙体厚0.10～0.20米，高0.51米。在西壁上砌筑一龛，宽0.22、高0.19米。顶部用两块石板搭盖而成，石板厚0.08～0.10米。双人并列合葬，头向42°，面向上，仰身葬。两头相靠，上身骨架较整齐，下肢叠放在一起。龛内随葬瓷罐1、瓷灯1。应为二次埋葬。从骨盆特征分析，左侧（61-1）应为男性，右侧（61-2）为女性，应为夫妻二次合葬墓。时代为明代（图三二；彩版三四，1～4）。

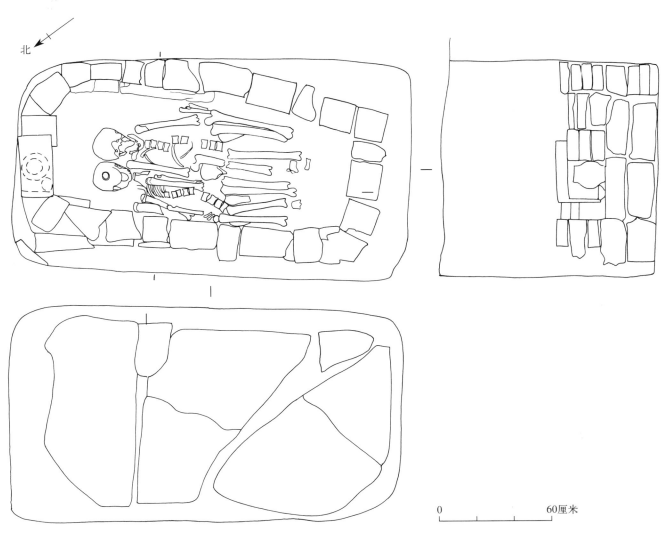

图三二（fig.32）　T1堆积61、62（M1）平、剖面图

第六章 出土遗物

一 建筑材料

建筑材料，有加工石材、砖、板瓦、筒瓦、瓦当、白灰墙壁等。

1．加工石材

共发现3块。

标本1，石板长37.0、宽18.0、厚10.5厘米。上下两面加工平整，凿刻斜条痕。

标本2，呈"L"形，石材长52.0、厚12.2厘米，一侧凿有槽口，宽4.5、深6.5厘米。上下面凿刻斜条形痕。

标本3，呈"L"形，石材长48.0、顶部宽5.5、底部宽11.0、高11.5、槽口宽4.2、深5.8厘米。顶面、底面、侧面及一端皆凿刻斜线痕。

2．砖

在遗址上用的砖多为泥质灰陶，个别的呈红褐色。砖的尺寸统一，长32.0～34.0、宽16.0、厚6.0厘米，一面有粗绳纹，另面平整光滑。堆积70中发现一块宽13.0、厚4.0、残长11.0厘米的青砖。

3．筒瓦

标本T435-70：11，瓦身略呈梯形，前端呈舌状子口，后端较直、外面抹光，内壁有布纹。长35.2、宽13.0～15.0、厚1.0厘米（图三三，1）。

标本T434-195：1，瓦身呈长方形，前端呈舌状子口，后端较直。长37.6、宽14.6、厚1.0厘米（图三三，2；彩版三五，1～3）。

4．板瓦

大而宽厚，呈一头窄的梯形。

标本T425-64：3，外面光滑，内壁有布纹，窄端较薄。长34.0～36.8、宽25.0～29.0、厚

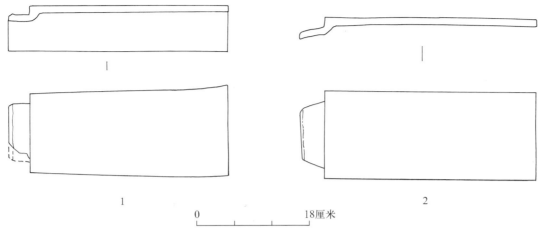

图三三（fig.33）　出土筒瓦
1、2. T435-70：11、T434-195：1

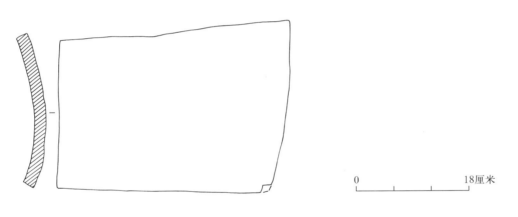

图三四（fig.34）　出土板瓦T425-64：3

2.0厘米（图三四；彩版三五，4、5）。

　　瓦规格是整齐划一的，应为一个大的时期统一制作的。在遗址的东北部发现有陶窑，应为就地取材建窑烧造的。

5. 瓦当

　　只有筒瓦有瓦当，材料与筒瓦和板瓦同，皆为泥质灰陶。外面的花纹用模子制作。共发现六种类型的瓦当。

　　A型　八瓣莲花瓦当，中间乳凸花蕾状心，花芯顶部弧凸，花瓣外侧有一周凸棱。外侧一周宽素缘高凸。花纹清晰规整。瓦当内侧面凹凸不平，有用手按捺痕迹。

　　标本T435-195：3，分开制作筒瓦与圆瓦当，然后对接加泥捏制而成。内有加泥手工捏制痕迹，外残存有对接缝隙痕迹。直径14.0～14.5厘米（图三五，1）。

标本TG1-15：8，瓦当内面有用手压抹痕迹。直径15.5厘米（图三五，2；彩版三六，1）

遗址上共发现42个比较完整的A型瓦当，堆积64中发现10个（彩版三六，2、3），堆积70中发现7个，堆积195中发现3个。

南墙之外的15号堆积，发现一个A型瓦当范模，标本TG1-15：25（彩版三六，4）。

B型　六瓣莲花瓦当。花瓣外周无凸棱，花蕊宽扁高凸。素缘高凸。花纹边角圆滑，不如A

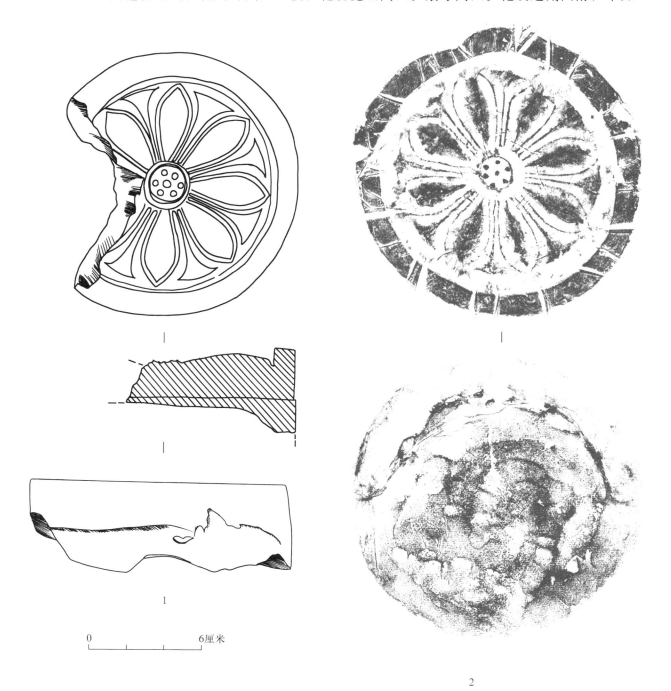

0　　　　　　　　6厘米

2

图三五（fig.35）　出土A型瓦当
1、2．T435-195：3、TG1-15：8

型清晰，应为模制形成。加工较为粗糙，烧制火候不均匀。瓦当内侧面不平，有手按捺痕迹。
直径14.0～15.5厘米。瓦当与筒瓦的连接有两种，一种同A型，标本T434-70：2（图三六，2）
和T434-70：12；一种单独制作瓦当，将外侧缘面去掉一半，把筒瓦黏贴在瓦当的外侧，标本
T433-70：15（图三六，1；彩版三六，5）。标本04ＸL200-201：4，直径15.7厘米（图三六，
3；彩版三七，1、2）。标本T434-179：7，直径16.2厘米（图三六，4）。

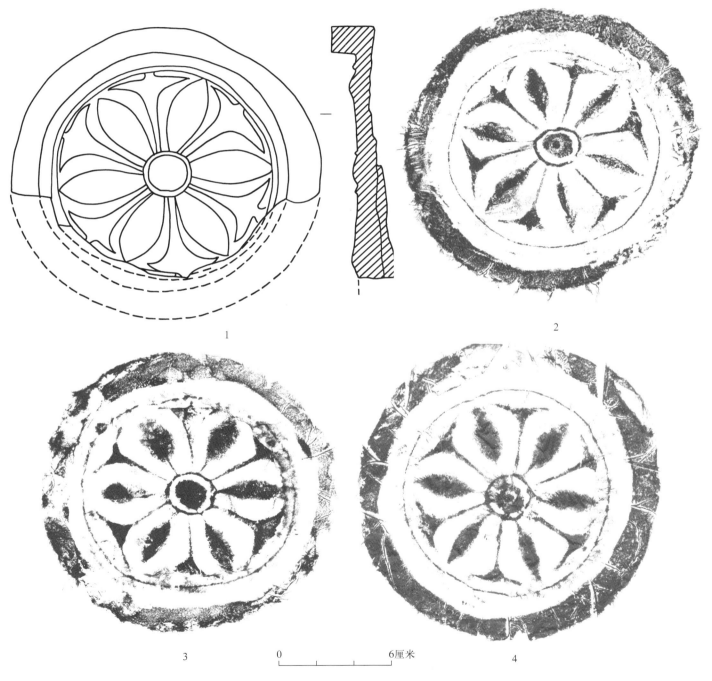

图三六（fig.36）　出土B型瓦当
1～4．T433-70：15、T434-70：2、04ＸL200-201：4、T434-179：7

　　B型瓦当共发现76个完整的，其中堆积64中发现一个，堆积70中发现34个，堆积195中发现3个，堆积69中发现2个。

　　C型　瓦当，花纹、尺寸同A型。只是花瓣间的花蕊顶部尖细。瓦当的背面不平，有手抹、捏制痕迹。筒瓦部分外侧圆弧面上可见瓦当和瓦身对接的线状缝。共发现2件。

　　标本T434-70：9，瓦身和瓦当分别制作黏接而成。直径约15.0厘米（图三七，1）。

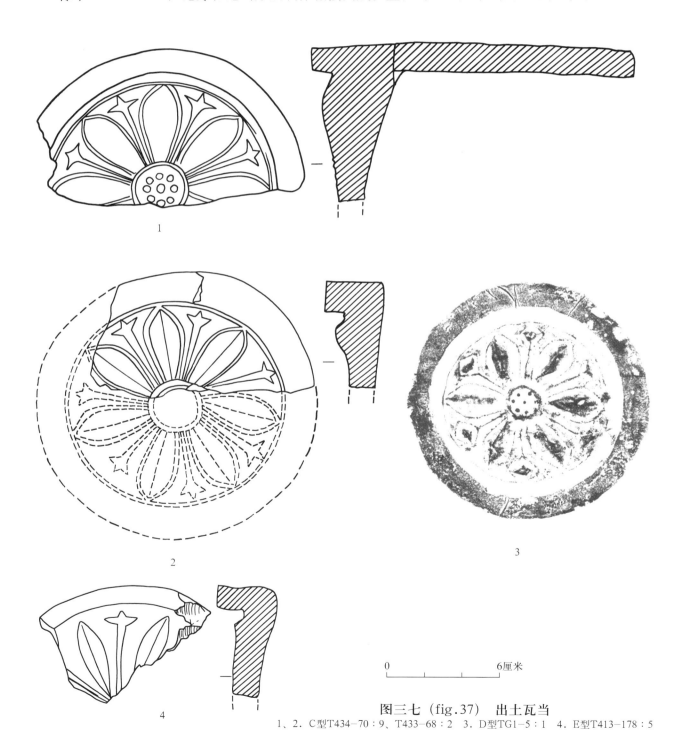

0　　　　　　　　　6厘米

图三七（fig.37）　出土瓦当
1、2. C型T434-70：9、T433-68：2　3. D型TG1-5：1　4. E型T413-178：5

标本T433-68：2，烧制完成，在瓦当正面的花瓣上间隔涂抹红彩和白彩。残长11.5厘米（图三七，2；彩版三六，6）。

D型　六瓣莲花，花瓣外有细凸棱。花蕊外有菱形细线凸棱围绕，下有细线凸棱状茎。莲蓬上模印8个凸点纹。仅发现一块。

标本TG1-5：1，瓦当较小，制法同A型瓦当。直径13.0厘米（图三七，3；彩版三七，3）。

E型　八瓣莲花，莲花瓣窄，花蕊茎较细，顶部较窄。缘面窄高。背面转角呈圆弧状。背面光滑，可见手抹痕迹，未见按捺痕迹。可能是在制作时下面有圆形底盘，上部用莲花内模印出莲花。仅发现1件。

标本T413-178：5，直径16.4厘米（图三七，4；彩版三七，4）。

F型　八瓣双瓣莲花，莲瓣宽厚弧曲，外有凸棱，凸棱前端尖而上翘。花蕊较短。中心莲蓬

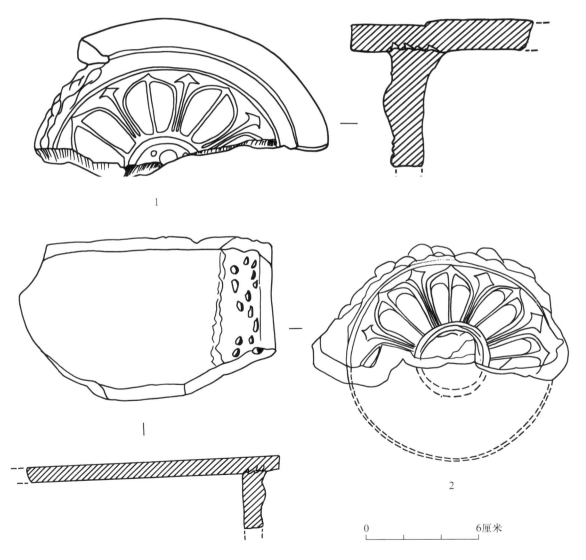

图三八（fig.38）　出土F型瓦当

1、2. T434-64：1、T434-70：17

较大，外两周凸棱。莲花外有一周凸棱。瓦当与筒瓦分开单独制作。瓦当外缘呈不规则乳突状凸起；筒瓦的前端内侧在制作时用尖状棍棒戳有许多深窝。瓦当和瓦身应该分两次制作完成，先制作筒瓦，瓦上戳孔，干后作瓦当黏贴在一起。复原直径16.0厘米，共2件。

标本T434-64：1，双瓣莲花宽扁肥厚，瓦当上涂有红色（图三八，1；彩版三七，5）。

标本T434-70：17，双瓣莲花较瘦高（图三八，2；彩版三八，1～4）。

二　陶　器

出土的陶器有泥质灰陶、黄褐陶、豆青陶以及夹细砂红陶等。纹饰以素面为主，另有弦纹、弧线纹、凸棱纹、附加堆纹、模印方格纹等。部分器物上发现钻孔修复的现象。器型有陶盆、罐口、罐系、瓮、瓶口、器盖、器口、盘等。

1. 陶盆

共20件。分为三型。

A型　6件。折沿盆。分为两亚型。

Aa型　3件。宽折沿，厚方唇。

标本T433-64：1，泥质黄褐陶。敞口，沿面下凹，沿折处一周凹槽，方唇宽厚下垂，唇面微内凹。斜腹，下内曲收，底部残。素面。上腹有一圆形钻孔，系器物破坏后修复用，孔径0.7、残高14.8厘米（图三九，1）。

标本T435-64：1，泥质灰陶。敞口，方唇较厚，唇面弧曲。沿折处一周凹槽，沿面微下凹。斜腹内收，底部残。上腹有一修复用钻孔，孔径0.6、残高8.4厘米（图三九，2）。

标本T434-70：25，泥质灰陶，泛青绿色。敞口，厚方唇，沿面微凹。上腹外曲，下腹内斜收，底部残。上腹外饰数道弦纹。残高12.0厘米（图三九，3）。

Ab型　3件。窄折沿，圆唇。

标本T423-5：1，泥质灰陶。敞口，厚圆唇，折沿下垂，沿面较平。腹部斜内收，下部残。残高9.6厘米（图三九，4）。

标本TG106-6：1，泥质灰陶，陶色泛青绿。敞口，折沿较窄下垂，沿面一周凹槽。斜腹内曲收，底部残。残高8.8厘米（图三九，5）。

B型　3件。卷沿，厚方唇。卷沿较宽，厚方唇。

标本T433-70：16，泥质灰陶，陶色泛青绿。敞口，厚方唇。宽沿下垂，沿面深下凹。曲腹，下部内斜收，底部残。上腹一修复用钻孔，孔径0.8、残高5.2厘米（图四〇，1）。

标本TG304-15：91，泥质灰陶，陶色泛青绿。敞口，斜方唇较厚，唇面内曲。沿较宽，沿面一周凹槽。曲腹下内斜收，底部残。残高6.4厘米（图四〇，2）。

标本T434-64：30，夹砂灰陶。敞口，厚方唇。卷沿下垂，沿面弧曲。下腹内曲收，下部

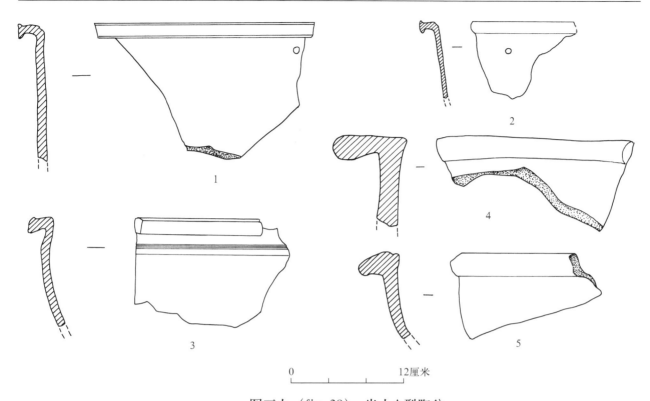

图三九（fig.39）　出土A型陶盆

1～3. Aa型T433-64：1、T435-64：1、T434-70：25　4、5. Ab型T423-5：1、TG106-6：1

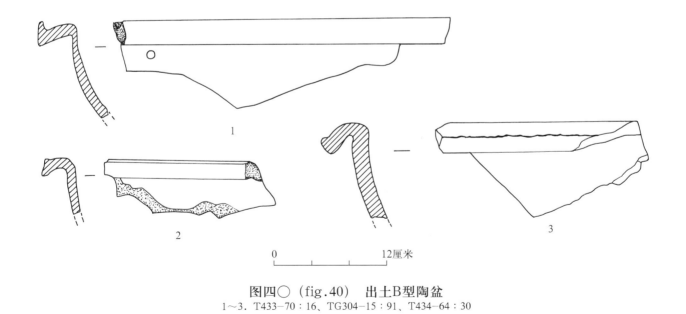

图四〇（fig.40）　出土B型陶盆

1～3. T433-70：16、TG304-15：91、T434-64：30

残。残高9.3厘米（图四〇，3）。

C型　共11件。卷沿，圆唇。均为泥质灰陶。分四亚型。

Ca型　5件。卷沿较窄，沿面较平。

标本T434-58：1，敞口，下腹内曲收，下部残。复原口径46.0、残高4.4厘米（图四一，1）。

标本T434-68：24，敞口，曲腹下内斜收，底部残。复原口径40.4、残高8.0厘米（图四一，2）。

标本TG106-5：2，口部微敛。沿面较厚。曲腹下内斜收。底部残。残高5.6厘米（图四一，3）。

Cb型　4件。卷沿，沿面斜下垂。

标本T4-C：1，敞口，曲腹下内斜收。内壁模印方格纹。残高3.9厘米（图四一，4）。

标本T434-198：10，口部微敛，曲腹下内斜收，底部残。复原口径32.8、残高7.6厘米（图四一，5）。

标本T434-139：6，敞口。尖圆唇，斜腹内收。底部残。残高6.0厘米（图四一，6）。

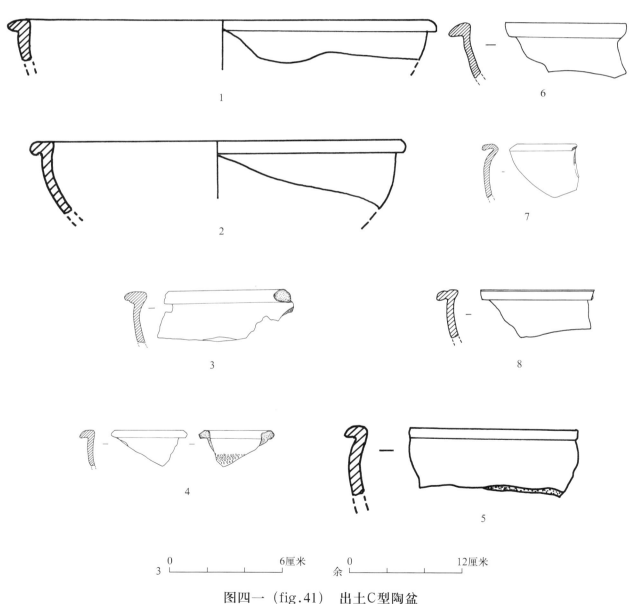

图四一（fig.41）　出土C型陶盆

1～3. Ca型T434-58：1、T434-68：24、TG106-5：2　4～6. Cb型T4-C：1、T434-198：10、T434-139：6　7. Cc型T434-68：3
8. Cd型T434-198：9

Cc型 1件。卷沿较宽，沿面弧曲。

标本T434-68：3，敛口，曲腹，底部残。残高5.9厘米（图四一，7）。

Cd型 1件。卷沿，沿面一周凹槽。

标本T434-198：9，敛口，曲腹下内斜收，底部残。残高5.2厘米（图四一，8）。

2．陶罐口

3件。分为两型。

A型 1件。

标本T434-70：24，泥质灰陶，陶色泛青绿。敛口，圆唇。宽斜沿，沿面斜平。束颈，鼓腹，下腹残。素面。复原口径19.8、残高7.2厘米（图四二，1）。

B型 2件。

标本424-118：1，泥质灰陶。敛口，厚圆唇，卷沿，沿面内弧。束颈，鼓腹，下部残。素面。残高4.8厘米（图四二，2）。

标本T434-68：23，泥质灰陶。敛口，厚圆唇。束颈，腹部外鼓，下部残。素面。复原口径33.0、残高10.0厘米（图四二，3）。

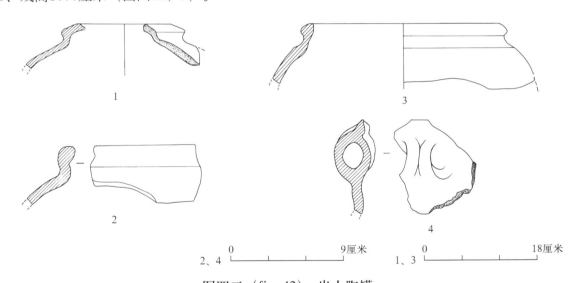

图四二（fig.42）出土陶罐
1．A型T434-70：24 2、3．B型424-118：1、T434-68：23 4．陶罐系T424-70：21

3．陶罐系

1件。

标本T424-70：21，泥质灰陶，陶色泛青绿。罐系呈牛鼻状。残高7.1厘米（图四二，4）。

4．陶瓮

共5件。分三型。

A型　共2件。卷沿，沿面有凹槽。

标本T435-64：2，夹砂灰陶。敛口，尖圆唇。束颈。大鼓腹，下部残。残高16.8厘米（图四三，1）。

标本TG304-15：96，夹砂灰陶。敛口，方唇。卷沿，沿面叠卷。大鼓腹，残。残高7.0厘米（图四三，2）。

B型　1件。窄卷沿，圆唇。

标本T434-198：11，敛口，泥质灰陶。大鼓腹。腹部有两组弦纹。残高12.0厘米（图四三，3）。

C型　共2件。沿向下翻卷，厚圆唇。

标本T434-64：29，夹砂褐陶。大鼓腹，残。残高6.6厘米（图四三，4）。

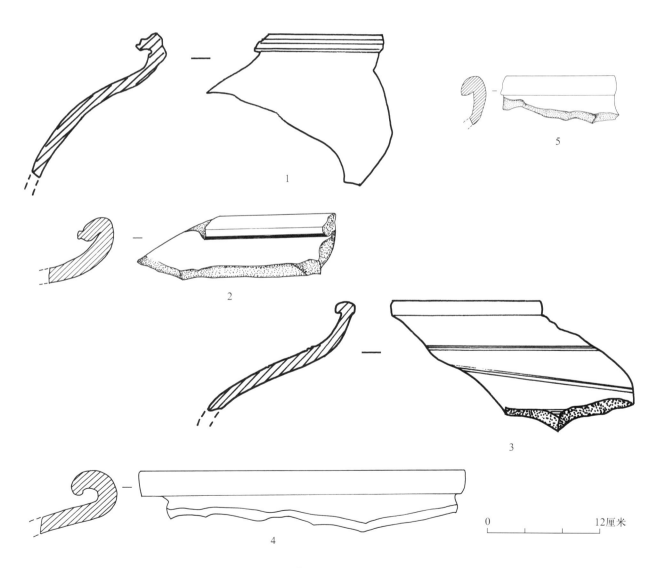

图四三（fig.43）　出土陶瓮

1、2．A型T435-64：2、TG304-15：96　3．B型T434-198：11　4、5．C型T434-64：29、T434-64：31

标本T434-64：31，夹砂褐陶。高束颈，大鼓腹，残。残高5.4厘米（图四三，5）。

5．陶瓶口

1件。

标本T434-64：26，泥质灰陶。盘状口，卷沿，厚方唇，唇面一周凹槽。高束颈，残。残高5.6厘米（图四四，1）。

6．器盖

1件。

标本T433-70：18，夹砂灰陶。敞口，圆唇，弧壁，顶部弧曲。口径6.9、高1.8厘米（图四四，2）。

7．陶盘

1件。

标本T434-64：35，夹砂红陶。敞口，圆唇，曲壁，平底。高3.4厘米（图四四，3）。

8．陶器口

2件。

标本T434-70：23，泥质灰陶，陶色泛青绿。敛口，方唇。折壁，上半部有数周高凸棱。下部内斜收。残高6.1厘米（图四四，4）。

标本T425-70：3，泥质灰陶。敛口，方唇。折壁，下部斜内收。口外饰戳印圆圈纹和两条一组的竖条纹，上半部饰一周高绳索状高凸棱。残高3.7厘米（图四四，5）。

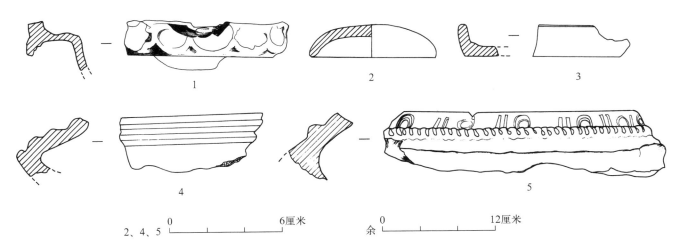

图四四（fig.44）　出土陶器

1．陶瓶口T434-64：26　2．陶器盖T433-70：18　3．陶盘T434-64：35　4、5．陶器口T434-70：23、T425-70：3

9. 附加堆纹陶片

3件。

标本T434-68：29，泥质灰陶。附加堆纹凹处可见按压痕迹。残高10.2厘米（图四五，1）。

标本T434-68：30，泥质灰陶。上饰一条绳索状附加堆纹。残高10.2厘米（图四五，2）。

标本T434-68：31，饰一条捺窝附加堆纹。残高13.0厘米（图四五，3）。

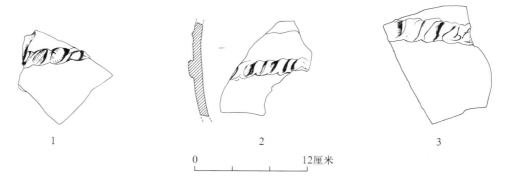

0   12厘米

图四五（fig.45） 附加堆纹陶片

1～3. T434-68：29、T434-68：30、T434-68：31

三 瓷器

有青瓷、白瓷、黑瓷、三彩等。青瓷有的胎质较差，杂质较多，釉呈豆青色，多杂黑斑点，外壁露胎，釉向下流淌。多数青瓷胎较纯，胎中泛青灰色，釉薄而亮。白瓷多泛青，胎土泛黄，较杂，釉面有冰裂纹现象。黑瓷釉面较薄。三彩仅见一件。器型有瓷碗、钵、盘、罐、壶、豆以及钻孔瓷片等。

1. 瓷碗

共30件。敞口，曲壁。分为四型。

A型 共14件。饼状足，底部平整。根据口部形状分两亚型。

Aa型 5件。大敞口，壁向外弧曲。

标本T434-70：26，白胎。外壁近足根处折平。足根刮削。内外施白釉，外壁半釉，下露白胎，釉面呈冰裂纹。内底部有三支钉痕。复原口径14.6、底径7.1、高4.5厘米（图四六，1）。

标本TG204-5：1，白胎略泛青。圆唇，饼状足较厚，足外撇，足根刮削。内外施白釉，外半釉，釉面呈细小冰裂纹。内底有支钉痕。口径13.5、足径4.6、高4.7厘米（图四六，2；彩版三九，1、2）。

标本T434-5：4，白胎。圆唇，饼状足较厚。内外施白釉，外壁半釉，露白胎。内底有三支钉痕。口径20.2、足径9.2、高6.0厘米（图四六，3；彩版三九，3）。

标本T434-70：3，黄褐胎。圆唇，外壁瓦楞状弧凸。内外施青釉，外半釉，下部露胎。内底

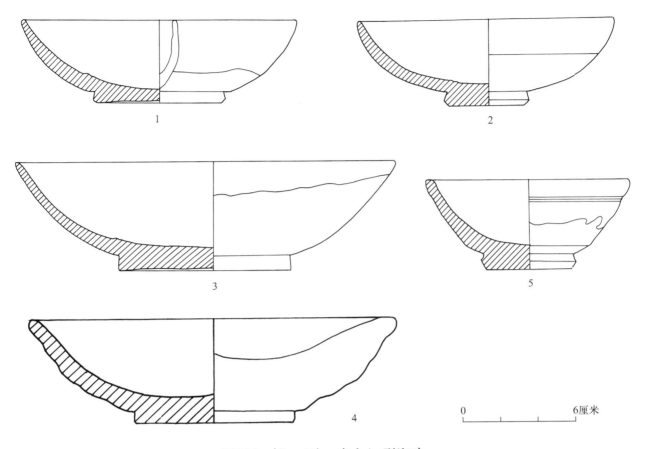

图四六（fig.46）　出土Aa型瓷碗
1～5. T434-70：26、TG204-5：1、T434-5：4、T434-70：3、T435-238：5

有三支钉痕。口径19.6、足径8.6、高6.0厘米（图四六，4；彩版三九，4、5）。

标本T435-238：5，灰白胎。厚圆唇。外壁上臂饰两周凸弦纹，外壁近足根处斜内收。饼状足较厚，足跟刮削。内外施青釉，外半釉，有流釉现象。口径10.9、足径5.1、高5.0厘米（图四六，5；彩版三九，6）。

Ab型　9件。外壁上部内曲收，上口部微外卷。

标本TG304-15：101，白胎，胎中泛黄，胎质较粗糙。碗底较厚，足跟刮削。施酱釉，内全釉，外壁半釉，有流釉现象，釉层较薄。复原口径14.8、足径6.0、高5.6厘米（图四七，1）。

标本T413-179：12，白胎。厚圆唇。施青釉，内全釉，外半釉。口径22.0、足径12.2、高6.2厘米（图四七，2；彩版四〇，1、2）。

标本T434-5：3，白胎。曲壁，上部外翻卷。底部较厚。施白釉，内全釉，外半釉，釉现青色。釉厚处有冰裂纹现象。口径15.4、足径6.0、高3.6厘米（图四七，3；彩版四四，4）。

标本TG206-44：1，灰白胎。碗底外部近平，足跟刮削。施青釉，内全釉，外半釉，下部露胎。釉中泛青绿色。口径13.1、足径5.4、高4.1厘米（图四七，4）。

B型　8件。饼状足心内凹。分三亚型。

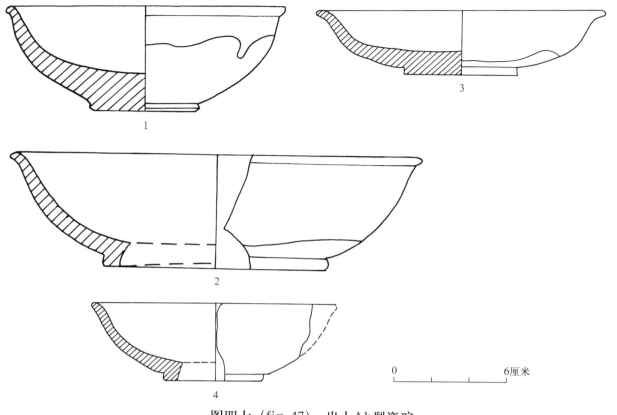

图四七（fig.47）　出土Ab型瓷碗
1～4. TG304−15∶101、T413−179∶12、T434−5∶3、TG206−44∶1

Ba型　4件。浅腹，大敞口，外壁曲壁。

标本T434−68∶2，白胎，胎中泛黄。圆唇较薄。足外撇，内施全釉，外壁半釉。内底三支钉痕。口径13.1、足径5.6、高3.9厘米（图四八，1；彩版四○，3、4）。

标本T2−64∶1，白胎。曲壁微弧曲。外壁底部近平。足外撇，足跟刮削。施白釉，内全釉，外壁半釉，下露白胎。内底有三支钉痕。口径16.0、足径6.8、高4.4厘米（图四八，2）。

标本T434−198∶5，圆唇较厚。外壁近底平。足外撇，足跟刮削。施青釉，内全釉，内底有三支钉痕，外壁半釉，露胎处有刮削痕。口径17.8、足径6.8、高6.2厘米（图四八，3；彩版四○，5、6）。

标本T433−5∶3，白胎。敞口，上部微内收。足外撇，足跟刮削。施白釉，外壁半釉，釉色暗青。口径13.9、足径7.3、高5.7厘米（图四八，4；彩版四一，1）。

Bb型　2件。浅腹，大敞口，外壁上部内曲。

标本T433−5∶2，白胎。外壁近底部平。足跟刮削。施白釉，内全釉，外壁半釉，内底有三支钉痕。口径19.2、足径9.0、高6.2厘米（图四九，1；彩版四一，2）。

标本T434−69∶103，白胎。足跟刮削，碗底较薄。施白釉，内壁全釉，外壁半釉，内底有三支钉痕。外壁露胎处有数周弦纹。口径18.6、足径8.8、高5.8厘米（图四九，2；彩版四一，3）。

Bc型　3件。深腹，口微敞。

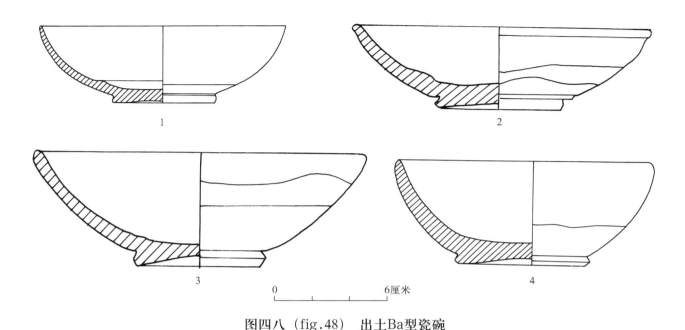

图四八（fig.48） 出土Ba型瓷碗
1～4. T434-68：2、T2-64：1、T434-198：5、T433-5：3

标本T434-199：6，厚圆唇。曲壁，外壁呈瓦楞状凸起，外壁近底部呈沟槽状内凹。足外撇，足跟刮削。外底上凹甚。内底较平整。施青绿釉，内壁全釉，外壁半釉，下露胎。口径14.2、足径7.4、高6.0厘米（图四九，3；彩版四一，4～6）。

标本T434-64：13，红褐胎。圆唇。曲壁，外壁呈瓦楞状弧凸。足外撇，足跟刮削。内底下凹。施褐彩。口径19.6、足径8.8、高7.8厘米（图四九，4；彩版四二，1、2）。

标本T435-70：18，白胎泛黄，胎质较粗。曲壁，饼状足，足跟外撇，足跟斜削，外底上凹，内底下凹，有三支钉痕。内壁及外壁上部施白釉。足径8.2、残高4.3厘米（彩版四四，5）。

C型 5件。玉璧底。仅存部分碗底。

标本T423-69：101，斜壁，足较矮，玉璧足外圈较宽，内底心呈尖状下凸。施白釉，内底三支钉痕，外壁釉至底。足无釉。足径5.1、残高2.0厘米（图五〇，1；彩版四二，3）。

玉璧底碗底还有标本T414-174：1（彩版四二，4、5）、T413-178：7、T425-195：15、T423-117：2（彩版四三，1～6）。

D型 3件。圈足。

标本T432-6：2，白胎。外壁近底部平。圈足跟微内斜。圈足较高。外底有一乳状凸。内壁施白釉，有砂钉痕。外壁露胎。足径6.2、残高2.8厘米（图五〇，2）。

标本T437-6：3，灰白胎。外壁近底平。圈足较高，微外撇。施黑釉，内底涩圈，外壁下露胎。足径5.6、残高3.0厘米（图五〇，3）。

标本T434-68：7，白胎细腻。大敞口，圆唇，沿下卷，曲壁。矮圈足。内外施白釉。口径14.4、足径5.4、通高4.5厘米（图五〇，4；彩版四四，1）。

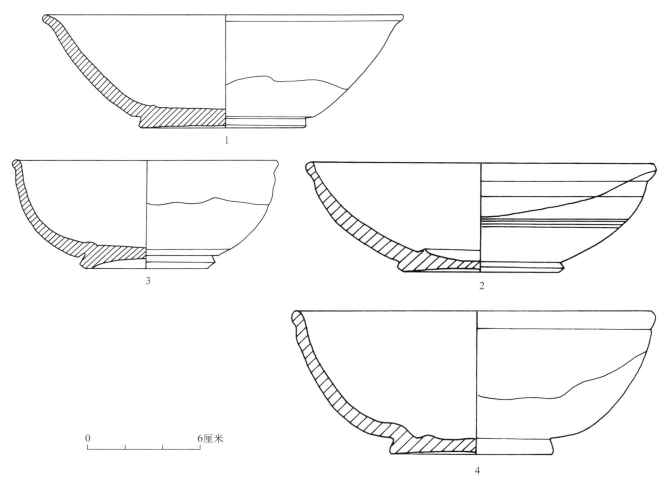

0　　　　　　　6厘米

图四九（fig.49）　出土瓷碗
1、2. Bb型T433-5：2、T434-69：103　　3、4. Bc型T434-199：6、T434-64：13

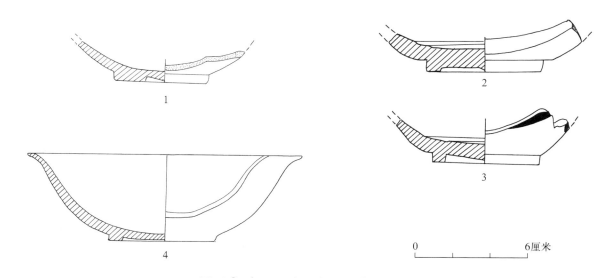

0　　　　　　6厘米

图五〇（fig.50）　出土瓷碗
1. C型T423-69：101　　2～4. D型T432-6：2、T437-6：3、T434-68：7

2. 瓷钵

共5件。分为两型。

A型 1件。口部微敛。

标本T434-198：1，白胎泛黄。敛口，圆唇。曲壁，上部外鼓，下腹内曲收。平底。内部施酱釉，外壁半釉，下部露胎。饰数周弦纹。口径11.7、底径4.4、高4.9厘米（图五一，1；彩版四五，1～3）。

B型 4件。口部内敛，鼓腹。

标本T433-70：19，白胎，胎中泛青。圆唇，口外一周凹槽。球状腹，底部残。通体施白釉，釉中泛青。外壁有露胎现象。口径11.2、残高7.3厘米（图五一，2；彩版四六，1、2）。

标本T435-238：6，尖圆唇。沿微外卷，球状腹。底部残。白胎泛青，外壁露胎处呈紫褐色。施豆青釉，内壁满釉，外壁半釉，有流釉现象。口径12.0、残高8.0厘米（图五一，3；彩版四六，3、4）。

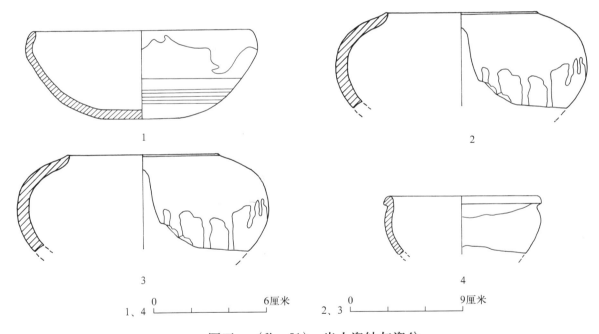

1   2

3   4

0   6厘米
1、4 ├──┼──┼──┼──┤

0   9厘米
2、3 ├──┼──┼──┤

图五一（fig.51） 出土瓷钵与瓷盆
1. A型瓷钵T434-198：1 2、3. B型瓷钵T433-70：19、T435-238：6 4. 瓷盆T434-69：106

3. 瓷盆

1件。

标本T434-69：106，白胎。口微敛，圆唇，沿外卷，沿下内束。曲壁下内斜收。底部残。内施白釉，外侧口部施白釉，下露白胎。残高3.2厘米（图五一，4）。

4. 瓷罐

8件。

标本T423-117：1，敛口，圆唇，颈部微内束，呈一周弧凸。鼓腹，下腹内斜收。底部残。复原口径11.5、残高6.5厘米（图五二，1）。

标本T413-BK：4，白胎。敛口，圆唇，鼓腹，上腹有双系。底部残。内施青釉，外壁上部施青釉，下露胎，泛红。外壁下半部有细弦纹。复原口径16.8、残高17.0厘米（图五二，3；彩版四七，1、2）。

标本T433-5：1，灰白胎。口微侈，厚圆唇，卷沿，颈部内束。鼓腹，腹鼓处略呈凹槽状。下腹斜曲内收。平底。圈足较矮，足根刮削，外底略内凹。内部施白釉，外壁上部白釉，下部露胎呈浅红色，有数周细弦纹。口径12.8、高9.2厘米（图五二，2；彩版四七，3、4）。

标本T434-5：5，灰白胎。敛口，厚圆唇。外侧一周高凸棱，束颈，鼓腹，残。通体施豆青釉，唇部无釉（芒口）。复原口径13.3、残高5.7厘米（图五二，4）。

标本T433-118：4，白胎，胎中泛黄褐色。仅存腹部。鼓腹，上有双条形系。施白釉，釉中泛青绿色。外壁半釉，有流釉现象。残高9.5厘米（图五二，5；彩版四七，5、6）。

标本T435-195：14，罐系。白胎泛青灰。双竖条形系。外表施酱黑釉。残高6.5厘米（图五二，6）。

标本T434-118：3，白胎。胎中泛黄褐色。鼓腹，系残，形状不清。内外施白釉，外壁半釉，有流釉现象。残高8.0厘米（图五二，7）。

5．瓷罐底

7件。分为三型。

A型　4件。平底，饼状足。

标本T434-139：7，白胎。鼓腹，上部内敛。平底，饼状足外撇，足根刮削。内壁满白釉，外壁半釉。底径9.3、残高7.5厘米（图五三，1）。

标本T433-70：20，红褐胎。鼓腹，下腹内曲收。饼状足，足根刮削，足底微上凹。残高4.0厘米（图五三，2；彩版四八，1~3）。

标本T433-5：7，灰胎。下腹斜内收。饼状足，足根刮削，底部平。内壁施黑褐釉，外壁露胎呈紫黑色。内壁有凸棱。底径9.0、残高4.5厘米（图五三，3）。

B型　2件。玉璧形底足。外底抠小圆形心。

标本T434-68：15，白胎。下腹斜收，足根刮削，底心呈乳状凸起。内壁呈凸棱状。内外施白釉，外壁半釉。足径9.5、残高9.8厘米（图五三，4；彩版四八，4~6）。

标本T434-68：4，白胎。斜壁内收。足根外撇。足外底抠圆形心，中部下凸。内外施白釉。足径7.5、残高4.2厘米（图五三，5）。

C型　1件。矮圈足。

标本T415-8：2，黄褐胎。鼓腹，下部内弧曲。圈足较矮，外底心刮削成浅心。底径12.6、残高6.0厘米（图五三，6）。

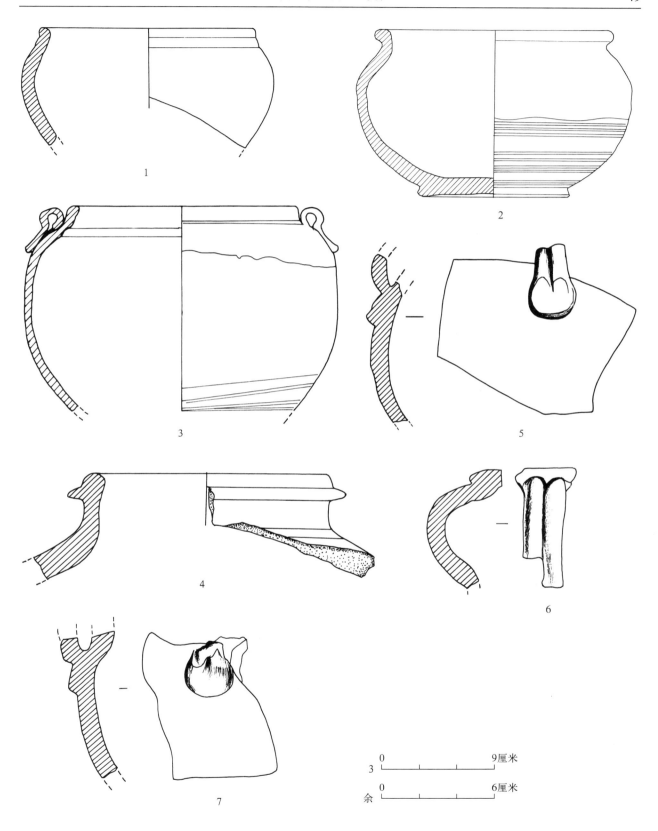

图五二（fig.52）　出土瓷罐

1～7. T423-117：1、T433-5：1、T413-BK：4、T434-5：5、T433-118：4、T435-195：14、T434-118：3

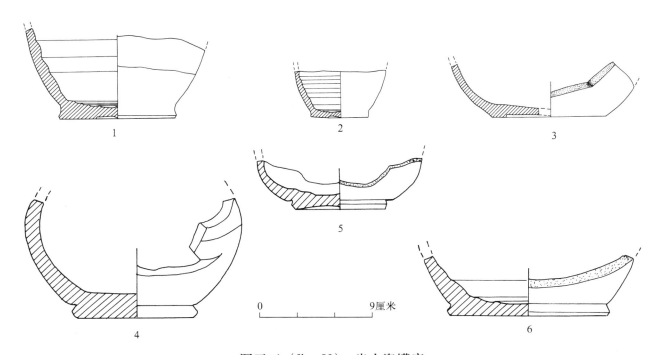

图五三（fig.53）　出土瓷罐底
1、2. B型T434-68：15、T434-68：4　3. C型T415-8：2　4～6. A型T434-139：7、T433-70：20、T433-5：7

6. 瓷壶

共6件。

标本T423-69：109，白胎。细高颈较直。口部残，外侧一周高凸棱状外凸。外壁施豆青釉，内壁上口部施釉。残高5.6厘米（图五四，1；彩版四九，1）。

标本T435-195：13，青灰胎。侈口，卷沿，圆唇。高束颈。鼓腹，肩部两周凸棱。通体施酱黑釉，釉色光亮。口径7.4、腹径11.8、残高8.0厘米（图五四，2；彩版四九，2）。

标本T434-198：8，白胎泛青灰。侈口，卷沿，圆唇，鼓腹，肩部一周凸棱。口径7.8、残高5.5厘米（图五四，3；彩版四九，3）。

标本T425-70：5，灰褐胎。敛口，鼓腹弧凸，短流。残高8.0厘米（图五四，4；彩版四九，4、5）。

标本T434-64：17，白胎泛黄。球状腹较瘦高，假圈足，平底。内壁及外壁上部施豆青釉，釉厚薄不匀。腹径12.6、底径6.6、残高10.2厘米（彩版五〇，1～4）。

标本T434-70：20，白胎泛青，胎质密而厚重。敛口，束颈，颈部一周凸棱。残高5.5厘米（图五四，5）。

7. 三彩豆柄

1件。

标本T434-64：14，白胎。高柄，下部外敞。外壁施黄、绿、褐三彩，色彩艳丽。残高15.0

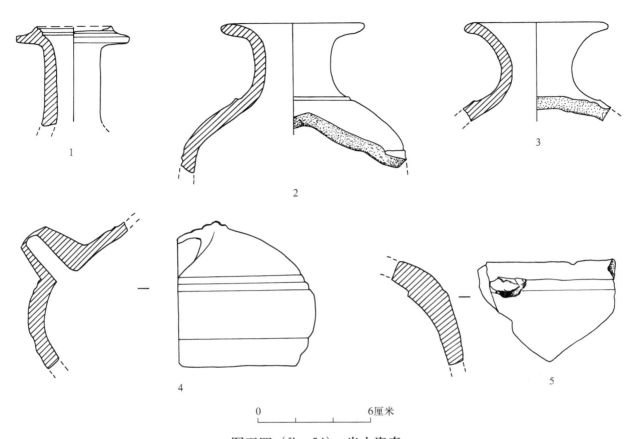

0　　　　　　　6厘米

图五四（fig.54）　出土瓷壶

1～5. T423－69：109、T435－195：13、T434－198：8、T425－70：5、T434－70：20

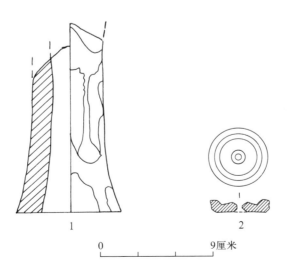

0　　　　　　　9厘米

图五五（fig.55）　出土器物

1. 三彩豆柄T434－64：14　2. 钻孔瓷片T435－70：17

厘米（图五五，1；彩版五一，1～6）。

8. 钻孔瓷片

共2件。在碗底钻孔而成。

标本T435-70：17，灰胎。在碗底部双面钻一圆孔，孔径0.4～1.0厘米（图五五，2）。

四　铁　器

铁器发现较多，有铁刀、弧刃刮刀、镰刀、锄、条形铁器、犁铧、锛、钉等。

1. 铁刀

1件。

标本T425-195：1，直背较厚，三角形刀身。刃部略残，两端残。残长19.1厘米（图五六，1）。

2. 弧刃刮刀

1件。

标本T434-68：6，弧形两面刃，宽3.8厘米。两侧呈弧曲状，柄的顶端呈圆棍形。高6.2厘米（图五六，2）。

3. 镰刀

1件。

标本T425-195：2，弧曲状镰身较宽，背部较厚，三角状镰头，刃部锋利。銎部残。残长16.4、宽2.9厘米（图五六，3）。

4. 铁锄

1件。

标本T425-141：1，宽直刃，残高10.5厘米。两侧弧曲。宽扁长方形銎，宽2.2、深3.6厘米（图五六，4）。

5. 条形铁器

1件。

标本T5-225：1，长条形，长14.3、宽4.2、厚2.2厘米。上端一侧有一宽扁凸棱，高0.7厘米（图五六，5）。

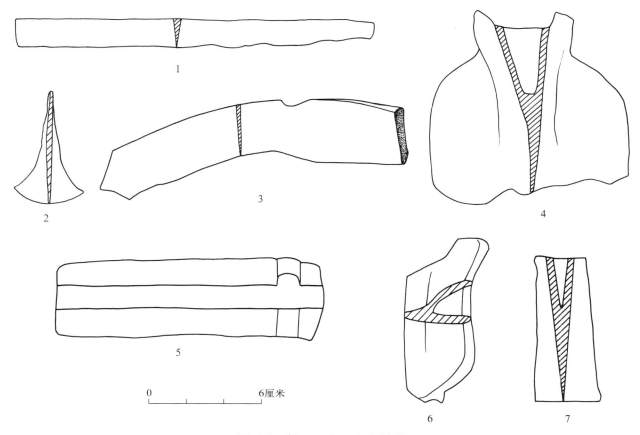

图五六（fig.56）　出土铁器

1．铁刀T425－195：1　2．弧刃刮刀T434－68：6　3．铁镰刀T425－195：2　4．铁锄T425－141：1　5．条形铁器T5－225：1　6．犁铧残块T434－118：2　7．铁锛T434－118：1

6．犁铧残块

1件。

标本T434－118：2，一侧成弧凸厚刃，另侧中空。残长9.0厘米（图五六，6）。

7．铁锛

1件。

标本T434－118：1，刃部略宽的梯形。刃部锋利，宽3.5、上部宽2.8、高8.0厘米。四棱长条状，銎口呈方形，宽0.9、深2.7厘米（图五六，7）。

8．铁钉

5件。分三型。

A型　3件。

标本T423－70：3，圆形帽较大，顶面弧凸，直径6.8厘米。四棱长条形钉身，较粗。长9.2厘米（图五七，1）。

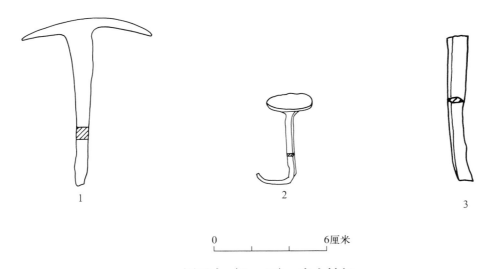

图五七（fig.57）　出土铁钉
1. A型T423−70：3　2. B型T425−191：1　3. C型T432−70：4

B型　1件。

标本T425−191：1，圆形帽较平，圆帽直径2.5厘米。方形四棱钉身，弯曲呈钩状。残高5.1厘米（图五七，2）。

C型　1件。

标本T432−70：4，四棱长条状顶身。长7.9厘米（图五七，3）。

五　铜　器

有铜钩、铜耳勺、铜带钩、铜钱等。

1．铜钩

1件。

标本ＴＧ203−29：1，细圆柱形柄，弯曲尖状细钩。高4.9厘米（图五八，1；彩版五二，1）。

2．铜耳勺

1件。

标本T434−68：1，宽扁柄，一面有凹状槽。圆形勺微前曲。长6.8厘米（图五八，2；彩版五二，2）。

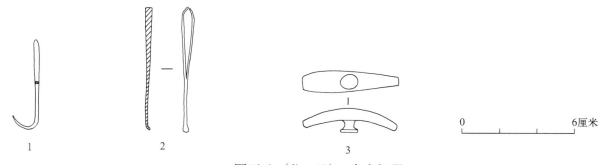

图五八（fig.58）　出土铜器
1. 铜钩TG203－29：1　2. 铜耳勺T434－68：1　3. 铜带钩T434－C：1

3．铜带钩

1件。

标本T434－C：1，圆形纽，弧曲带钩。残长5.3厘米（图五八，3）。

4．铜钱

共发现6枚。

五铢钱　3枚。皆为宽缘，五字斜划较直，铢字金字头内斜，朱字横弯曲。为隋代五铢钱。

标本TG105－15：13，直径2.2、穿长0.8厘米（彩版五二，3、4）。

开元通宝　1枚。

标本T434－68：1，一侧缘较窄，似打磨。直径2.3、穿长0.7厘米（彩版五二，5）。

乾元重宝　1枚。

标本T434－1：1，直径2.4、穿长0.8厘米（彩版五二，6）。

小钱　1枚。

标本TG103－33：1，文字不清。直径1.7、穿长0.7厘米。

六　骨　器

共2件。有骨锥、骨管等。

1．骨锥

1件。

标本T434－70：13，用长骨加工而成。尖部打磨光滑，较锋利。后半部呈凹曲状。后端宽扁。长11.5厘米（图五九，1；彩版五三，1、2）。

2．骨管

1件。

标本T413-181：1，用圆形长骨加工而成。两端切割磨光。中空。高3.5厘米（图五九，2）。

七　角器

鹿角

共3件。

标本T423-118：3，上端一角用锯锯掉。高17.1厘米（图五九，3；彩版五三，3、4）。

标本T423-118：2、1，从角的根部锯断（图五九，4、5；彩版五三，5、6）。

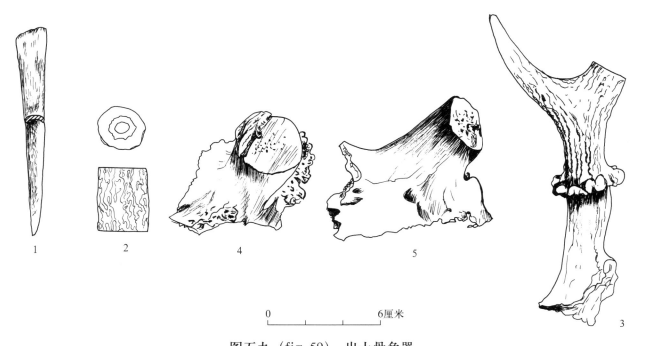

图五九（fig.59）　出土骨角器

1. 骨锥T434-70：13　2. 骨管T413-181：1　3～5. 鹿角T423-118：3、T423-118：2、T423-118：1

八　佛教造像

白龙寺遗址发掘出土了200余件石头造像残块和9件陶塑像残块。在发掘工作开始之前，村民在河边修路时发现了几十件造像残块，其中的26件被临朐县博物馆和考古发掘队收藏。

遗址出土有石头造像残块、白陶塑像、灰陶塑像，多为残块，部分保存较好，以石造像为主。遗址发掘前，从百姓手里采集到的佛造像皆为石造像，编号用C。

1. 石造像

石造像共发现200余件，多为残块。有单体佛造像、单体菩萨造像、背屏式造像、造像台座等。

标本ＴG3-15：17，背屏造像残块，绿泥石片岩。高度15.0厘米。残存背屏三尊造像的主尊佛及右侧胁侍菩萨，头部残，下有榫。主尊佛圆肩宽厚，身材高大。内着圆领衫，外穿褒衣博带式袈裟，下穿宽大长裙下垂至脚面，裙角外展。手施无畏、与愿印，左臂上搭宽帛垂于体侧，跣足立于圆台上。右侧胁侍菩萨流肩，上着交衽衫，下穿长裙下垂至脚面，裙角外展。着天衣，披帛横扎腰间、交于腹前、上绕腕部下垂身体两侧，圆形饰可能为玉璧；跣足立于圆座。用平直刀法雕刻而成，较为粗糙。背屏后打磨光滑，阴刻铭文三行十字"（普）泰二年（公元532年）」…赵鸳女」…敬造供養"（图六〇，1～3；彩版五四，1、2）。

标本ＴG3-15：13，背屏造像残块，绿泥石片岩。残高12.0厘米。为背屏式三尊造像，仅存主尊足部、外裙下摆、圆台和榫。用平直刀法雕刻而成。背面打磨光滑，阴刻铭文，残存"世"和"西"二字。复原尺寸大于标本ＴG3-15：17，造型与之相类，应同为北魏晚期造像（图六一，1、2；彩版五四，3、4）。

标本ＴG202-217：1，背屏立佛造像残块，石灰岩。高度21.0厘米。头部、台座插榫、背屏残。圆肩较窄，身穿褒衣博带式袈裟，身前曲波形衣纹下垂，衣脚外展。下着长裙至脚面。跣足立于圆台上。左手施与愿印，右手残。后侧背屏平整光滑。用平直刀法雕刻。为北魏晚期造像（图六八，2；彩版六〇，2、3）。

标本ＴG304-15：56、15，菩萨头部残块，高度8.2厘米。石灰岩。从残存部分分析，应为背屏式造像的胁侍菩萨残块，仅存头部。头戴花冠，冠带垂至耳旁，额前梳3个圆形发饰，面颊丰满，嘴露微笑。风化严重。应为北魏晚期到东魏时期造像（图六〇，4；彩版五五，1）。

标本ＴG304-15：69、70，单体菩萨残块，石灰岩。残高15.0厘米。仅存菩萨头的下半部。脸部肥硕圆润，下颌丰满，鼻梁高隆，鼻角宽大。嘴角内收，双唇较薄，笑嘴轻合，大耳宽厚，冠带下垂于耳后。平直刀法雕刻而成。从头的后侧看，没有背屏，是一个单独供养的菩萨。从脸部形态观察，和青州龙兴寺所出非常相似，应为北魏末期或东魏造像（图六〇，5；彩版五五，2）。

标本ＴG304-15：35，背屏造像残块，石灰岩。残高26.0厘米。仅存佛像胸部一段。弧曲形衣纹下垂。用平直刀法雕刻而成。为北魏末到东魏时期造像（图六二，2、3；彩版五五，5）。

标本ＴG304-15：14，背屏造像残块，石灰岩。高度21.0厘米。仅存佛像下身一段。着褒衣博带式袈裟，中部衣纹成圆弧形下垂，两侧衣纹斜直，裙角弯曲折皱，层次分明。衣裙下摆外展。背部较平，应有背屏。用平直刀法雕刻而成。为北魏末年到东魏时期造像。从造型风格和雕刻手法来看，与标本ＴG304-15：35应为同一座佛像残块（图六二，4、5；彩版五六，1）。

标本ＴG105-15：73，单体菩萨立像残块，石灰岩。高度8.0厘米。仅存菩萨中部一段。薄衣，弧形衣纹下垂，饰高浮雕穗状缨络，背面呈弧形凸起，阴线雕刻竖条形衣纹。为北魏末到东魏时期造像（图六四，1、2；彩版五七，1）。

标本ＴG304-15：34，背屏造像莲花座，石灰岩。残高13.0厘米。为佛像莲花座，三面高浮雕雕刻单层双瓣仰瓣莲花。莲座背部残，无莲花。莲花座下雕刻有莲茎。用平直刀法雕刻而成。

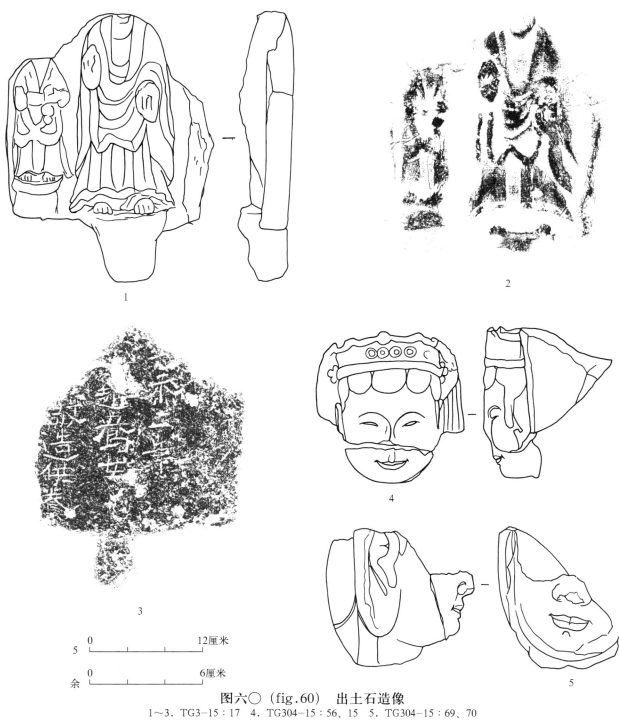

图六〇（fig.60）　出土石造像

1～3. TG3-15：17　4. TG304-15：56、15　5. TG304-15：69、70

上部残。为北魏末期到东魏时期造像（图六四，3、4；彩版五七，2）。

　　标本TG304-15：24，背屏造像残块，石灰岩。残高10.5厘米。正面刻五圈圆环形头光，背面存阴线刻衣纹。用平直刀法雕刻。为北魏末年至东魏时期造像（图六五，4、5；彩版五八，2）。

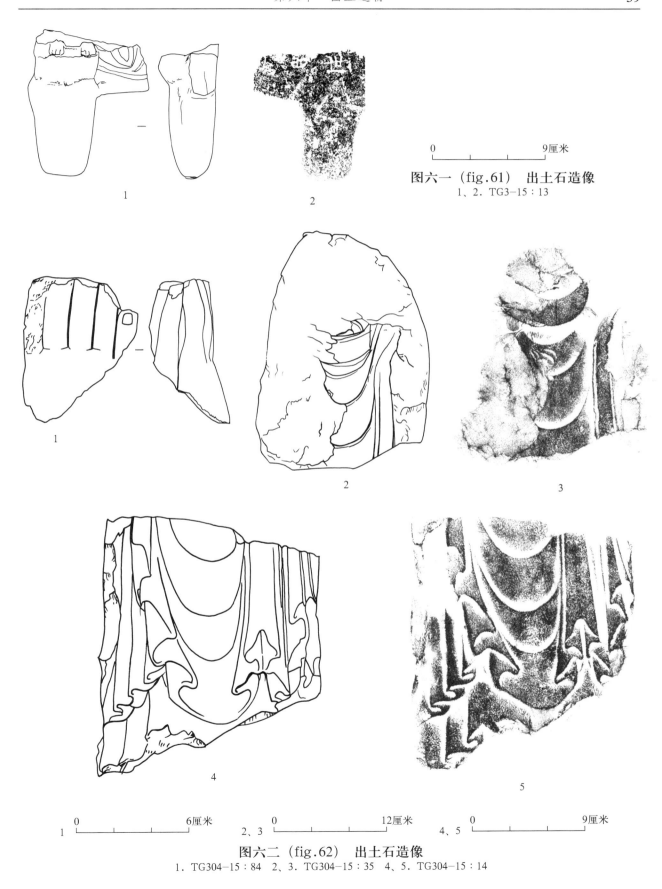

图六一 (fig.61)　出土石造像
1、2. TG3-15：13

图六二 (fig.62)　出土石造像
1. TG304-15：84　2、3. TG304-15：35　4、5. TG304-15：14

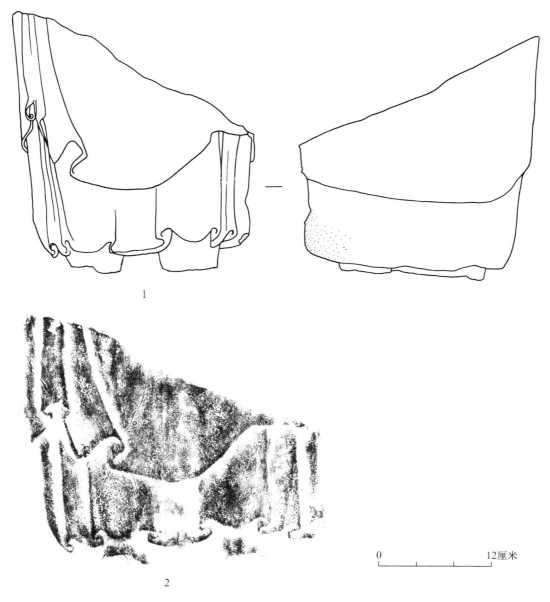

图六三（fig.63）　出土石造像
1、2. TG105-15：6

　　标本路基US：1，背屏造像残块，石灰岩。残高5.0厘米。正面雕刻五圈圆环形头光。用平直刀法雕刻。该残块和TG304-15：24发现位置不同，但从外型、风格和雕刻手法来看，应为同一座造像的背屏。为北魏末年至东魏时期造像（图六五，6；彩版五八，3）。

　　标本TG304-15：53，圆台残块，石灰岩。残高22.0厘米。仅存圆台、双脚局部。双足瘦长，脚趾纤细。跣足立于圆台上。为北魏末年至东魏时期造像（图六六，3）。

　　标本T434-195：11，造像残块，石灰岩。残高6.6厘米。仅存造像的右手臂。右臂上抬紧靠身体。右手竖立，四指弯曲，拇指直立轻捏食指旁。肥大袖口从手臂自然下垂。手部残存鎏金。为北魏末年到东魏时期造像（图六七，2）。

标本TG304-15：81，单体立佛残块，石灰岩。高度5.0厘米。用平直刀法雕刻而成。左手施与愿印。为北魏到东魏时期造像（图六七，3；彩版五七，5）。

标本TG204-15：79，造像残块，石灰岩。残高8.0厘米。仅存造像的左手，手施与愿印。宽大衣袖从臂上自然下垂。为北魏末年到东魏时期造像（图六七，4；彩版五九，2）。

标本TG304-15：28，石灰岩，残高7.0厘米。仅存造像的左手，左手下垂，手指纤细，手掌向前，施与愿印。宽大衣袖从臂上下垂。为北魏末年到东魏时期造像（图六七，5；彩版五九，3）。

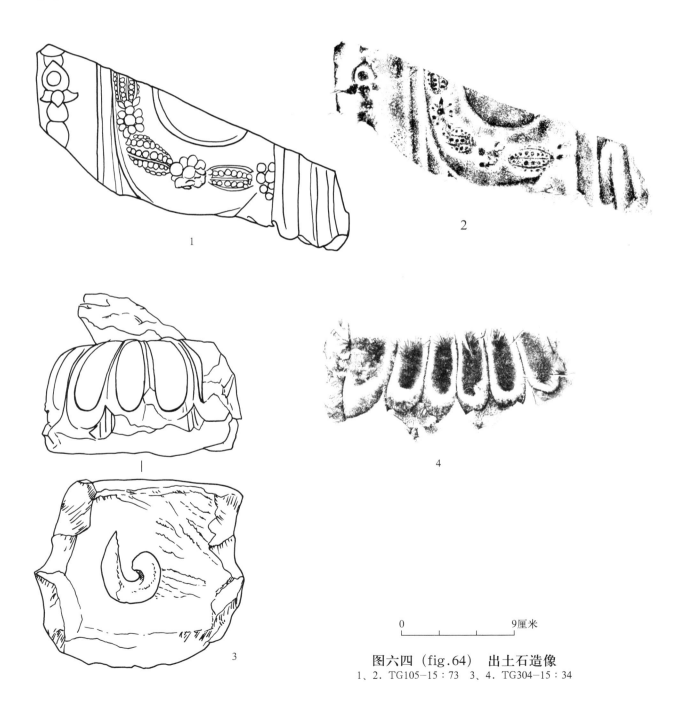

0　　　　　　9厘米

图六四（fig.64）　出土石造像
1、2. TG105-15：73　3、4. TG304-15：34

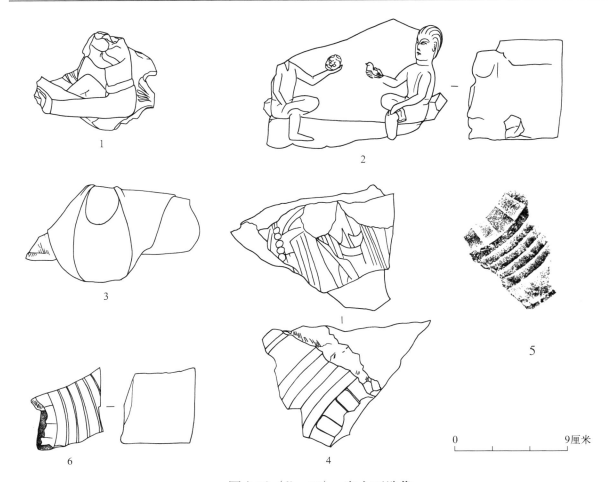

0   9厘米

图六五（fig.65） 出土石造像
1. TG304-15：62 2. TG304-15：23 3. TG304-15：49 4、5. TG304-15：24 6. 路基US：1

标本TG304-52、53：1，佛像残块，石灰岩。高度30.0厘米。胸部一段，内着圆领衫，外衣衣纹下垂。背部平整，应为背屏造像残块。为北魏末至东魏造像（图六九，3、4）。

标本T414-BK：4，造像残块，滑石。高度9.0厘米。石头夹杂绿色斑点，石质松软，用指甲能够刻划。在一面用刀具深刻衣纹，有的衣纹向下深透，已经刻好；而有的衣纹没有刻到位置就停住，下面还保存原来石料，没有进行加工。应为造像的半成品。从加工刀法和残存衣纹分析，为北魏至东魏造像（图七一，1；彩版五七，6）

标本TG202-216：1，造像头光残块，石灰岩。高度16.0厘米，头光复原直径46.0厘米。右侧佛像站立莲花上。头部残。圆肩肥厚，内着斜衽衫，外穿较薄的肥袖佛衣，双手合于胸前。下穿长裙。佛像周围雕刻莲花枝叶。用平直刀法雕刻。头光的背面凹凸不平，中部残存一较深的梯形刻槽，宽1.5～3、深2.2厘米，为修复痕迹。为东魏造像（图六八，1；彩版六〇，1）。

标本TG304-15：16，造像残块，粉沙岩。高度14.5厘米。仅存右手局部。宽袖下垂，纤手露出。手背肥厚滋润，小指、无名指伸展，中指、食指微屈，拇指下伸，残，似素手轻拢拿捏东西。手心涂红彩，手背残留施彩痕迹。平直刀法和圆润刀法结合雕刻而成。应为东魏至北齐造像

图六六（fig.66） 出土石造像
1～4. TG304-15：4、TG304-15：45、TG304-15：53、TG304-15：65

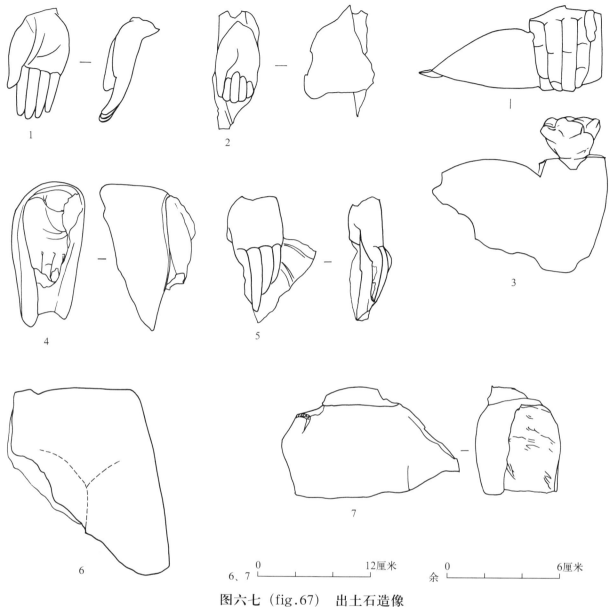

图六七（fig.67）　出土石造像

1～7. TG304－15：90、T434－195：11、TG304－15：81、TG204－15：79、TG304－15：28、TG105－15：5、TG304－15：77

（彩版五五，3）。

　　标本TG105－15：6，单体立佛像残块，石灰岩。残高29.5厘米。仅存佛像下肢部分残块。薄衣裹体，下着贴体长裙，外披曲边自然下摆袈裟。背面显露衣裙双层，佛衣下摆呈弧边形，下露贴身裙。用圆润刀法雕刻而成。为北齐时期造像（图六三，1、2；彩版五六，2、3）。

　　标本TG304－15：62，背屏造像残块，石灰岩。残高8.0厘米。仅存背屏上部飞天之局部。飞天挺身直坐，左腿向前直伸，脚下蹬圆形物，右腿弯曲侧立。手臂上举，头、手残缺。人物丰满，肌肤感觉清楚。背屏镂空雕作花形。为北齐时期造像（图六五，1；彩版五七，3）。

　　标本TG304－15：23，石灰岩，残高10.5厘米。下部雕刻双层长方形台座，底部残，座残宽

12.0、厚7.0厘米。正面高浮雕雕刻有两个人物，呈半跏趺坐式侧身对坐于台上。右侧人物较完整，昂头挺胸，发髻呈长辫状后梳，垂于脑后。长脸肥硕，弯眉细目向左前侧视，大鼻隆起，小嘴微翘。左腿斜搭台下，右腿盘于左腿上，左手按在腿上。右手持一瑞鸟向前递伸。左侧人物略显清瘦，头部残，身微前倾。右腿斜搭于台上，右手按在右腿上，左腿横搭在右腿上。左手托一

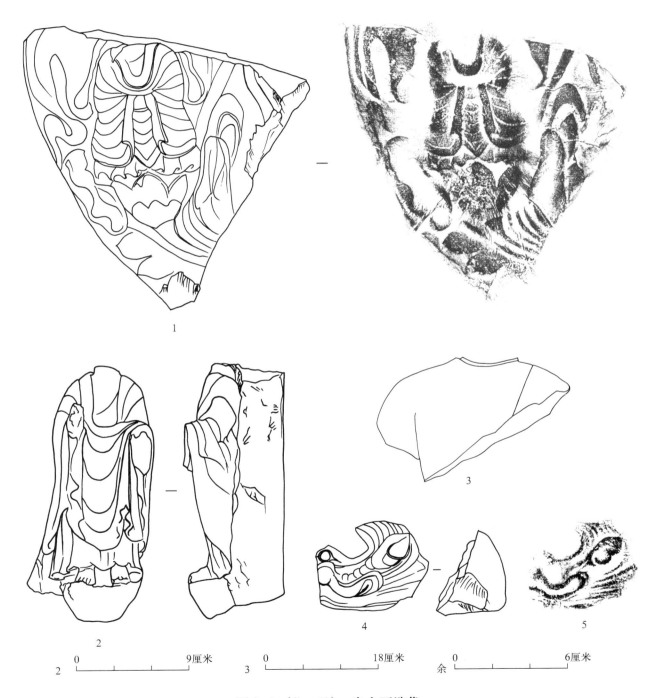

图六八（fig.68）　出土石造像

1. TG202-216：1　2. TG202-217：1　3. TG304-15：33　4、5. TG304-15：98

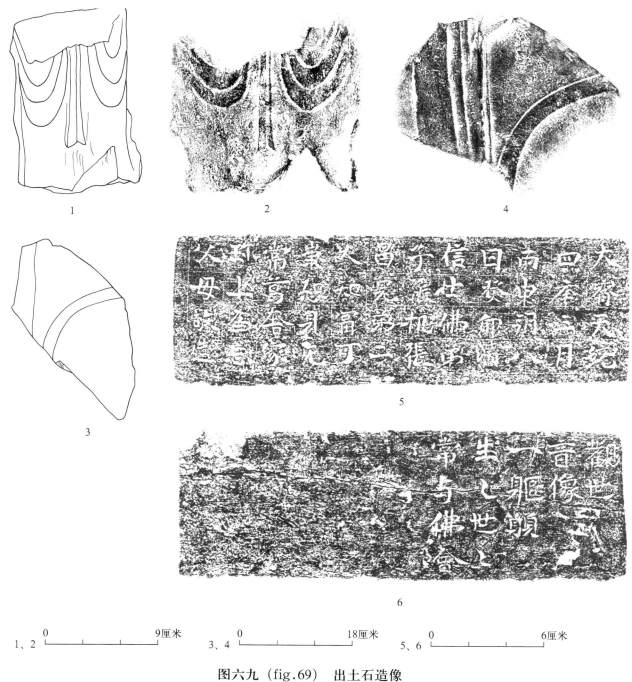

图六九（fig.69）　出土石造像
1、2. TG304-56、57：1　3、4. TG304-52、53：1　5、6. T434-69：1

人头（头骨），与右侧人对举。两侧面台上各雕刻一圆钮状饰，长约0.9厘米。后面上部打磨光滑，下部刻台座。顶部残。为北齐时期造像（图六五，2；彩版五七，4）。

　　敦煌壁画中常见一人手捧小鸟、一人手捧骷髅，有人说是鹿头梵志和婆薮仙。有的学者怀疑这种说法。

　　标本TG304-15：49，造像残块，石灰岩。残长14.0厘米。可能是横抬于胸前的小臂残块，上雕有衣纹。为北齐时期造像（图六五，3；彩版五八，1）。

标本ＴＧ304-15：4，单体立佛造像残块，石灰岩。残高23.0厘米。仅存圆形台、佛的左脚。小腿粗壮，脚背肥厚圆润，脚趾栩栩如生，形同真人大小，反映造像个体较大。台下残存榫。为北齐时期造像（图六六，1；彩版五八，4）。

标本ＴＧ304-15：45，单体立佛造像残块，石灰岩。残高16.0厘米。仅存圆形台、双脚。跣足立于台上。长脚纤趾，脚背肥厚，圆润光滑，呈现肌肤之美感。为北齐时期造像（图六六，2；彩版五八，5）。

标本ＴＧ304-15：65，圆台残块，石灰岩。残高13.0厘米。仅存脚、台的局部和榫。脚背肥硕，脚趾肥润。榫外表面有凿痕。为北齐时期造像（图六六，4；彩版五八，6）。

标本ＴＧ105-15：5，立佛造像残块，石灰岩。高度20.0厘米。仅存佛像腰腿部分。小腹微凸，秀腿长立。下着轻薄衣裙紧贴身体，隐约可见身体形态。为北齐造像（图六七，6；彩版五九，4）。

标本ＴＧ304-15：77，立佛造像残块。石灰岩。残高12.0厘米。仅存造像胸部。胸部肥厚弧凸，北部宽厚健美。身着贴体薄衣，身体形态隐约可见。为北齐造像（图六七，7；彩版五九，5、6）。

标本ＴＧ304-15：33，佛像残块，石灰岩。高度20.0厘米。仅存胸部。左肩着袒右衫，身体右侧裸露，圆肩浑厚，胸部肥硕，肌肤滋润，极现人体之美。为北齐造像（图六八，3；彩版六〇，4）。

标本Ｔ434-69：1，造像底座，石灰岩。正方形底座，宽24.5、高8.5厘米。顶部微下凿，宽16.0厘米。侧面打磨光滑，细线阴刻方格底线，前面和左侧面阴刻63个字：“大齊天統」四年三月（公元568年）」丙申朔八」日癸卯清」信士佛弟」子張机張」昌兄弟二」人知富可」崇恐身无」常葛（割）舍家」珍上为忘（亡）」父母敬造」觀世」音像」一軀願」生生世世」常與佛會。”正面每行4个字，侧面每行2~4个字（图六九，5、6；彩版六〇，5~7）。

标本ＴＧ304-56、57：1，立菩萨像，石灰岩。高度15.5厘米。菩萨的下半身，天衣呈圆弧形下垂，衣带垂至腿部。裙子紧贴双腿。背部圆弧形外凸，为独立菩萨像。为北齐造像（图六九，1、2；彩版六〇，8）。

标本ＴＧ305-58：2，佛像头部残块，石灰岩。高度7.0厘米。佛螺发。眼睛微睁，低眉垂目斜视下方。面颊肥润，大耳下垂。为北齐造像（图七〇，1；彩版六〇，9）。

标本ＴＧ304-15：84，造像残块，石灰岩。残高8.0厘米。仅存手部。手指纤长，手指微曲，双手合十，手背肥厚，残。略有风化，时代不详（图六二，1；彩版五五，4）。

标本ＴＧ304-15：90，造像残块，石灰岩。残高6.0厘米。仅存造像的右手。竖掌直立，手掌肥厚，掌心纹路清晰，手指微曲，五指轻拢，形态温柔。掌前侧雕刻精细，肌肤感觉明显。背面加工粗糙。应为北朝造像（图六七，1；彩版五九，1）。

标本ＴＧ304-15：71，立佛造像残块，石灰岩。高27.0厘米。仅存造像腿部后面部分。可见

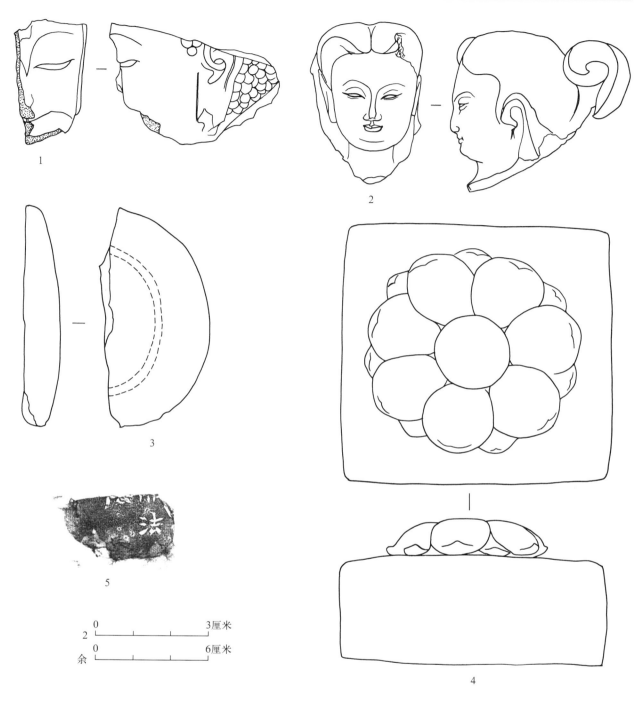

图七〇（fig.70）　出土石造像
1. TG305−58：2　2. TG305−58：1　3. T414−12：2　4. T414−12：1　5. T434−181：5

下体内衣、外衣痕迹。为北齐造像。与标本15：77，造像风格及残存大小、形状一致，可能为同件造像残留。

　　标本堆积TG304−15：98，龙头残块，石灰岩。高度5.0厘米。龙的脖子和嘴已残。仅存龙的长嘴、大眼和巨耳，毛发卷扬。龙头前侧及后面打磨光滑，应为镂孔透雕而成（图六八，4、5）。

标本ＴG305-58：1，飞天头像，石灰岩。高度4.5厘米。长发后梳，顶部微分，两缕细发垂至耳前。高额细眉，眼睛微睁，头向右侧，斜视下方。高鼻隆起，小嘴微笑，两腮肥美。满脸恬静和蔼。头后施旋形装饰。为北朝造像（图七〇，2；彩版六一，1、2）。

标本T414-12：2，造像头光残块，石灰岩。高度12.0厘米。呈中部较厚边缘略薄的圆饼状。正面加工平整光滑，残存一周圆环形底彩，可能为用颜料绘画或贴金形成头光。头像残。背部凿长方形卯孔，为修复痕迹（图七〇，3；彩版六一，4、5）。

标本T414-12：1，方台莲花座，石灰岩。方形台，宽14.5、高6.0厘米。上面雕刻单瓣覆莲圆形座，高2.1厘米，中间有一卯孔，径4.2厘米（图七〇，4；彩版六一，8、9）。

标本T434-181：5，铭文残块，石灰岩。宽6.0厘米。在光滑面上用阴线刻方格网，内阴刻造像题记，残存3字，2字不清。"……法"，应为铭文的最后两行（图七〇，5）。

标本T413-BK：1，为造像背屏残块，石灰岩。高33.0厘米。背屏右侧部分，雕刻同心圆环形头光，外圈阴线刻植物花纹带。外侧残存五周同心圆环背光边缘。为平直刀法雕刻。背面阴线刻细线纹图案，内容不清。为北朝造像（图七二；彩版六一，6、7）。

标本C：123（SLF656），"比丘宝□"造像背屏残块，石灰岩。残高25.0厘米。为造像碑左上角一部分。正面磨光，阴线刻佛和菩萨头光的局部，菩萨的头光内饰莲瓣纹；旁边饰圆形花状纹、火焰纹；上方残存一高浮雕飞天的部分。背面刻有铭文，残存七行，保存17个铭文"比丘宝□（爽？）……」大魏孝昌……」五日壬……」法社□（政？）……」三老……」孙……」□……"。为北魏造像（公元525～527年）（图七三，3～5；彩版六三，4、5）。

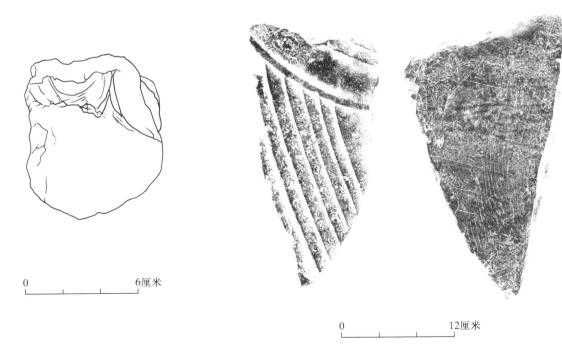

图七一（fig.71）　出土石造像T414-BK：4　　　图七二（fig.72）　出土石造像T413-BK：1

标本C：125（SLF660），背屏造像残块，石灰岩。高44.0、厚14.0厘米。存背光的左上侧，左侧保存较好。头光残，存四周圆环纹。背光顶部中间雕刻一飞龙，口衔莲枝与头光外圈纹带相连接，左侧雕刻一飞天，昂头挺胸，弯腰屈腿，怀抱一莲苞状物，火焰状帛带飞扬，似与龙飞行翱翔空中。其后存一飞天飞舞的帛带。与青州北魏太昌元年惠照造弥勒像（青州香港展p154的广饶张谈造像碑图6～9）内容同，为北魏晚期造像（图七四，2、3；彩版六三，6）。

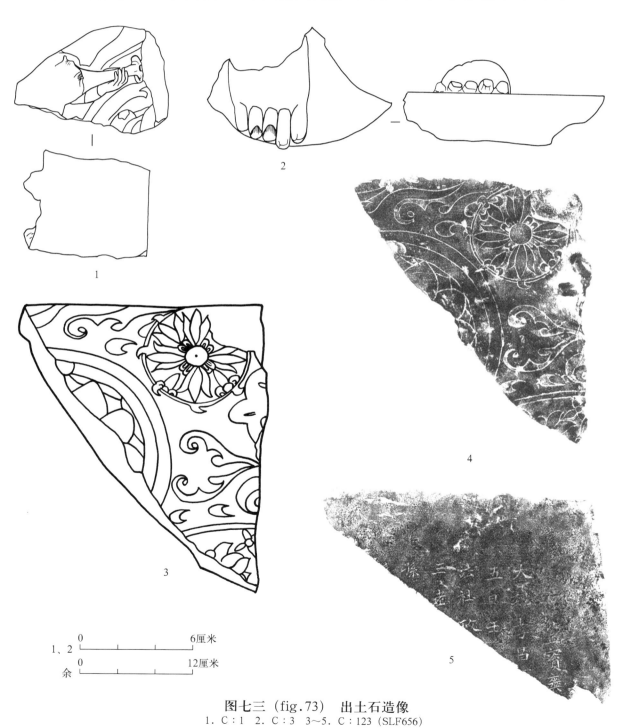

图七三（fig.73）　出土石造像
1. C：1　2. C：3　3～5. C：123（SLF656）

标本C：117（SLF613），背屏造像残块，石灰岩。高度6.5厘米。正面存阴线刻三周圆环头光和三周椭圆形背光。背面印刻铭文，残存二行七字"……兴和二年……」……丁丑朔……」……"。为东魏造像（兴和二年为公元540年）（图七四，1，七六，5；彩版六四，5、6）。

标本C：114，立菩萨像，石灰岩。高度39.2厘米。为背屏式三尊造像的左侧胁侍菩萨。高冠垂缯，小嘴细目，脸部圆润。佩项圈，内着斜衽衫，腰部衣带结扎，长带下垂及膝，带上系花结，长裙掩足。身穿天衣，身体两侧垂至台下。右手施无畏印、左手施与愿印。跣足立于台上。右侧背屏上可以看出龙的腿、尾残留。为东魏北齐造像（图七四，5；彩版六四，4）。

标本C：110（SLF658），背屏三尊造像残块，石灰岩。高度34.0厘米。主尊跣足立在圆台上，上部残损。左侧胁侍菩萨立在仰莲台上。其间雕刻一游龙，龙头高抬，口衔莲台，曲身卷尾，双爪捂在两侧台侧。佛像台座上残留另条龙爪。龙的颈部和足部为镂孔透雕。应为北齐造像（图七六，4；彩版六五，3）。

标本C：120（SLF609），菩萨立像残块，石灰岩。高度25.0厘米。仅存菩萨腰部以下部分。长裙下垂，裙纹呈之字形折皱下落。外穿天衣，从腹部圆环内交结穿过，绕行下垂身体两侧。身佩缨络，在腹部交结下垂至身体两侧，绕行体后。为北齐造像（图七六，1～3；彩版六六，1、2）。

标本C：118，单体立像，石灰岩。高度19.5厘米。为站立的单体佛像腰部一段。束腰细腿，着薄衣，体形隐现。右手上横端，宽帛搭在臂上垂于体侧。为北齐造像（图七九，2；彩版六七，5）。

标本C：1，造像背光残块，石灰岩。高5.5厘米。仅存飞天左手上握琵琶，两侧衣带飞扬。背部平整光滑。应为北朝造像（图七三，1；彩版六三，1、2）。

标本C：3，造像右脚残块，石灰岩。宽度10.0厘米。脚背肥厚圆润光滑，脚趾细长，站立圆形台座上。台座背面残破处，风化损害严重（图七三，2）。

标本C：101，莲花座，石灰岩。高度20.5、直径42.0厘米。侧面雕刻三层覆莲瓣，莲座顶部有八角形浅槽安放造像用。底座内部凿空，莲座侧壁厚4.0～6.0厘米（彩版六三，3）。

标本C：115（SLF612），佛头像，石灰岩。高37.2厘米。肉髻高凸，头前部饰螺发，头两侧条形长发下垂，脑后未雕刻头发。细眉弯曲，大眼半开，向前平视。鼻梁高隆，鼻角宽厚，小嘴轻合，微笑怡然。肥脸大耳，面颊肥硕。颈下残。县博物馆从百姓手中收藏。应为东魏到北齐时期造像（图七四，4；彩版六四，1～3）。

标本C：122（SLF658），背屏造像残块，石灰岩。高度40.4厘米。残存背屏中间一部分，五周圆环形身光，外侧一周凸棱，其间饰植物纹带。左侧残留龙尾和胁侍菩萨衣服。背面浅浮雕一组三个人物，衣纹用阴线细刻。中间站立一僧人，圆脸大耳，头微前倾。身着宽肥僧衣，内着长裙及足。手捧圆盒。左侧一僧人，身穿肥大僧衣，手托圆盘，侧身站立。右侧刻一方形座，上刻莲花，莲花座上坐一人，仅存右臂，可能为二僧人供奉的佛像。应为北朝造像（图七五，

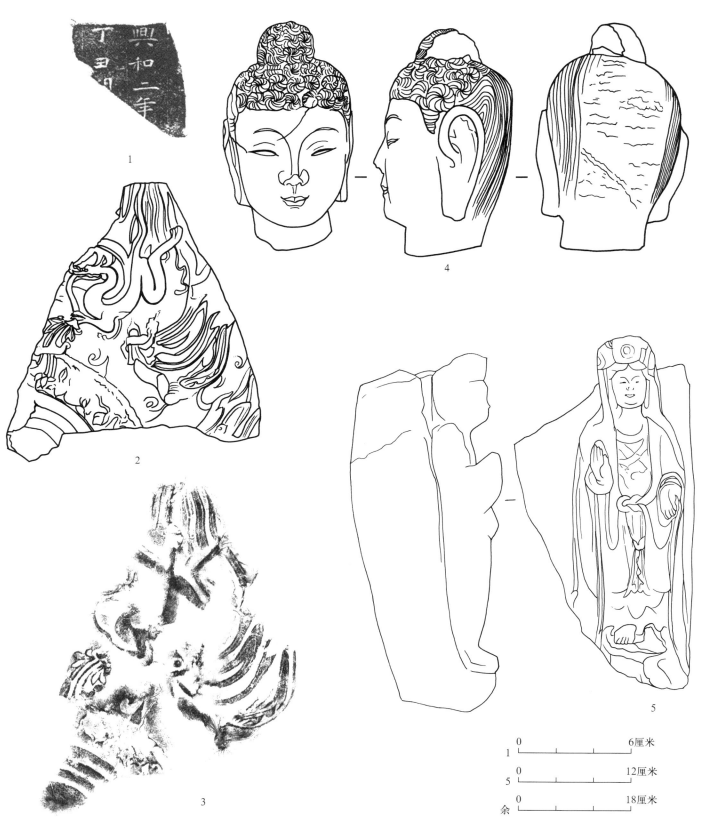

图七四（fig.74）　出土石造像
1. C：117　2、3. C：125（SLF660）　4. C：115（SLF612）　5. C：114

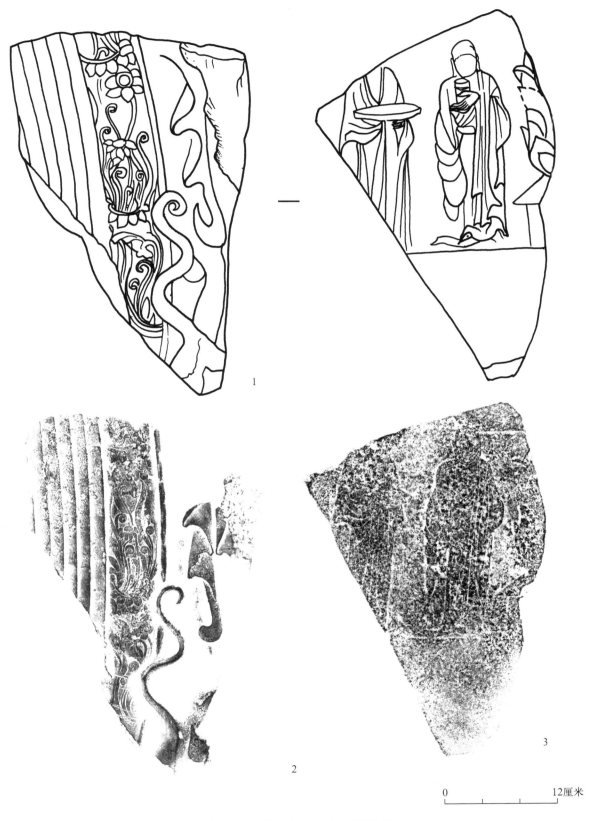

图七五（fig.75）　出土石造像
1~3. C：122 (SLF658)

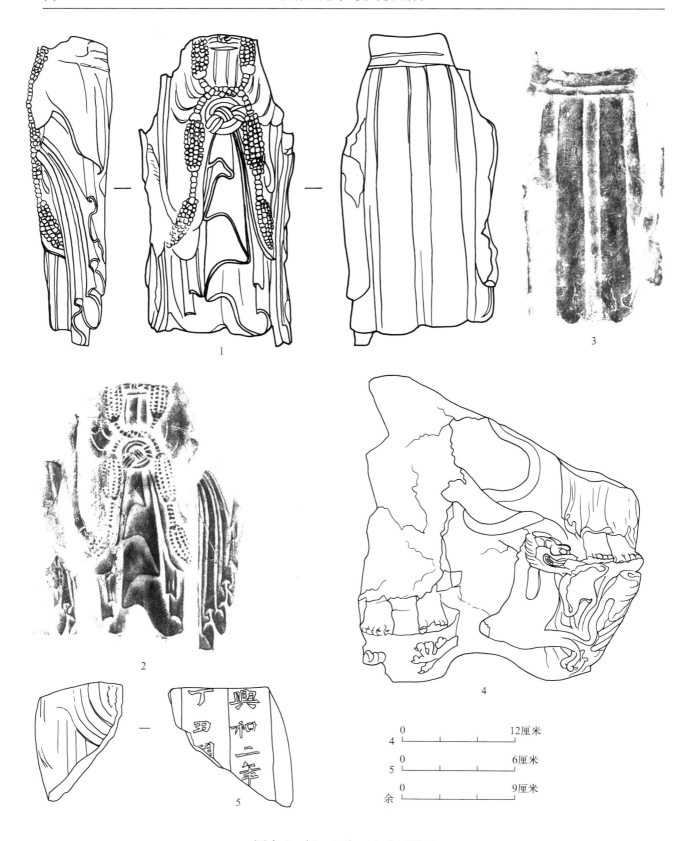

图七六（fig.76）　出土石造像
1～3. C：120（SLF609）　　4. C：110（SLF658）　　5. C：117（SLF613）

1～3；彩版六五，1、2）。

标本C：109（SLF627），背屏造像残块，石灰岩。高度40.0厘米。高浮雕雕刻龙、莲花。三只龙爪开张有力，身腿矫健，龙头高昂，眼睛圆瞪，须发飞扬，龙嘴开启，口中吐出莲花，应该上托莲座。应为北魏晚期到东魏时期造像（图七七，1、2；彩版六六，4、5）。

标本C：121（SLF662），背屏造像残块，石灰岩。高10.0厘米。为背屏造像主尊右侧身光残块。佛的身光阴线雕刻，为五周圆环，左侧为莲花纹带，右侧刻植物纹带，其右刻二道细线。上方刻圆形头光，饰莲花纹。右上方浅浮雕刻菩萨莲瓣头光。左侧佛像毁坏。应为北朝造像（图七七，3、4；彩版六五，4）。

标本C：124（SLF654），背屏造像残块，石灰岩。高度20.0厘米。为主尊与胁侍菩萨的局部。正面打磨光滑，用阴线刻细线纹和高浮雕的莲花纹。图案分为两组，一组为主尊头光部分的浅浮雕莲瓣和六道阴线圆弧纹，背光部分的莲瓣纹、弧线纹带、荷莲纹带、忍冬花纹；胁侍菩萨头光部分的阴线圆弧纹。与121纹饰与雕刻技法相同，可能为同一工匠加工而成。为北朝造像（图七七，5、6；彩版六五，5）。

标本C：107（SLF71），莲花座，石灰岩。高14.5、直径30.0厘米。圆形台，双层双瓣莲座，高浮雕刻而成。圆台侧面上阴刻铭文，共13行、52字"故人王口苻」妻石男口」故人王宝林」故人惠明」妻焦男口」林妻李绯？」……"施主（捐款人）有三个男主人、四个妻子、六个孩子（图七八，1、2；彩版六七，6）。

标本C：116（SLF70），"孙文"造像莲花座，石灰岩。高23.0厘米。方形台，宽27.5、高15.0厘米。上部高浮雕雕刻双层单瓣莲花，中心有圆形榫孔以插造像用，孔径7.5厘米。方台侧面打磨光滑，阴线雕刻六行32字"□平七年四月」八日孙文敬造」□潘为亡息阿」□造像一躯□」□□生天□□」□福」"。应为武平七年（公元576年）（图七八，3、4；彩版六七，1、2）。

标本C：108，莲花座，石灰岩。高度21.0厘米。圆形台，上为高浮雕双层单瓣莲花座。上有卯孔以插造像用。应为北朝造像（图七八，5；彩版六七，3）。

标本C：111，背屏造像残块，石灰岩。直径14.5厘米。仅存背屏造像圆形头光部分，前面的头部被砸掉。头光的边缘有的部分光滑完好，间隔一段存砸破痕迹，可见头光应为镂空雕刻而成，在山东地区仅发现这样一件，制作方法复杂，颇具地方特色。应为北朝造像（图七九，1；彩版六七，4）。

2. 白陶塑像

标本T413-70：5，菩萨立像，白陶。高7.5厘米。头部和圆台榫部残。圆肩束腰，长腿玉立，右手执莲蕾上于胸前，左手执一物贴于体侧，双脚赤裸站在圆台上。上身裸，佩项圈，双肩披帛（天衣），绕至腋下垂至身体两侧。缨络斜交于胸前。下着长裙，外套短裙，衣带结扎腰部。背面有指纹按捺痕迹，为范内捏塑而成（根据推测，左手应举莲蕾，右手持净瓶）。应为北齐塑像（图八〇，1、2；彩版六二，1）。

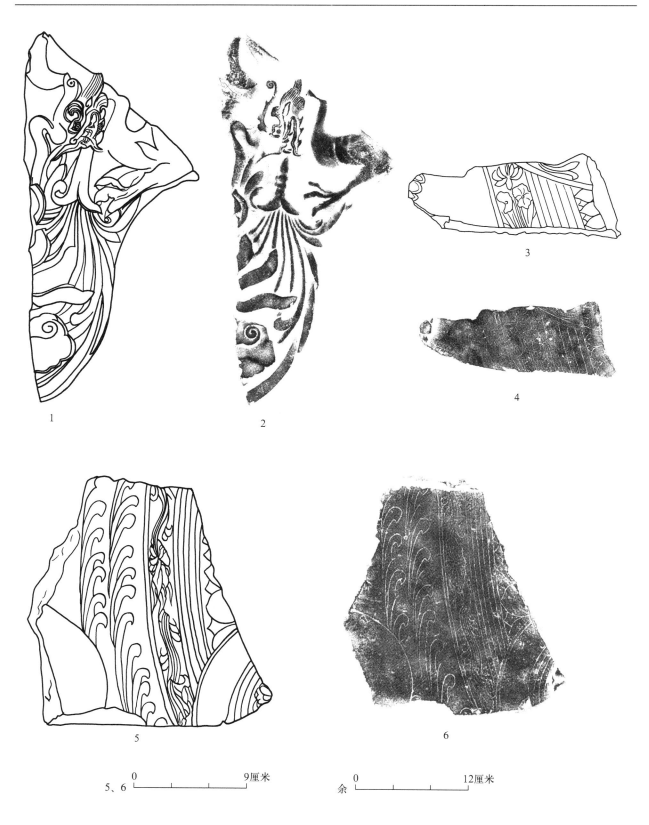

5、6 |0———————9厘米

余 |0———————12厘米

图七七（fig.77） 出土石造像
1、2. C：109（SLF627） 3、4. C：121（SLF662） 5、6. C：124（SLF654）

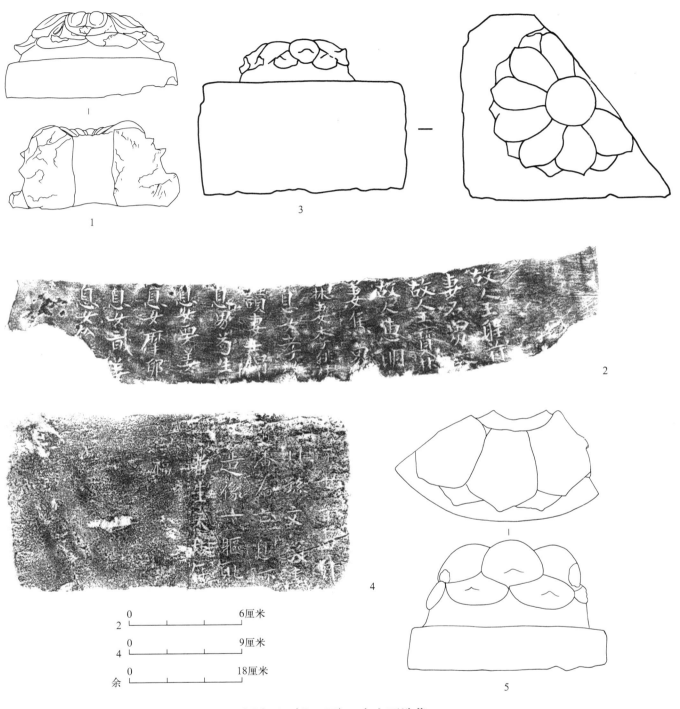

图七八（fig.78）　出土石造像
1、2．C：107（SLF71）　　3、4．C：116（SLF70）　　5．C：108

　　标本T414-74：2，菩萨立像残块，白陶。残高5.5厘米。仅存下半身。着长裙，天衣（披帛）垂至腿侧。双脚赤裸站在圆台上。背面有按捺指纹，为范内捏塑而成。应为北齐塑像（图八〇，3；彩版六二，2）。

　　标本T413-181：4，莲花座，白陶。宽4.0厘米。双层方形台，台高1.4厘米，上作双瓣覆莲

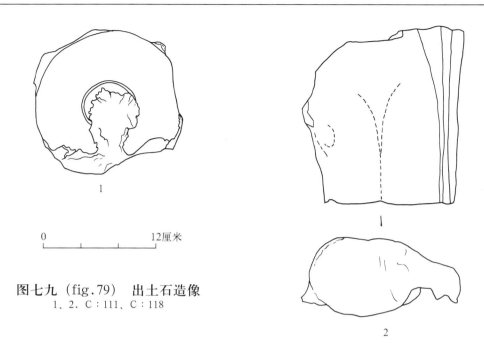

0　　　　　　　　　　12厘米

图七九（fig.79）　出土石造像
1、2．C：111、C：118

座，中间有圆孔。在范内捏塑而成（图八〇，5；彩版六二，5）。

标本TG304－C：1，莲花座，白陶。仅存一面，残高2.6、残宽3.6厘米。上为圆形，仅有二瓣覆莲，下为双层叠涩台（彩版六二，4）。

3．灰陶塑像

标本T413－178：2，灰陶莲座。高度19.5厘米，复原直径78.0厘米，壁厚12.0厘米。莲座呈底小口大中心空的圆圈状，底部平，上部残。外侧饰四层向上的莲花叶，每个叶宽度10.0厘米。用夹砂泥土手工捏制烧造而成。应为当地陶窑烧造（图八〇，4；彩版六一，3）。

标本T434－201：6，坐佛残块。泥质灰陶。残高7.5厘米。头部残。内着祖右衫，左肩斜披袈裟。双手施与愿印，结跏盘坐在圆台上。胳膊、双腿形态肥厚。背靠舟形屏，凸棱状椭圆形背光，背屏周边饰植物形纹饰。屏背面弧凸。用手捏制烧造而成，造型简单随意，可能为唐代塑像（图八〇，6；彩版六二，3）。

图八〇（fig.80）出土陶质塑像

1、2. 白陶像T413-70：5　3. 白陶像T414-74：2　4. 灰陶像T413-178：2　5. 白陶像T413-181：4　6. 灰陶像T434-201：6

第七章　分期与年代

一　瓷器与陶器

遗址发现的瓷器有青瓷、白瓷、黑瓷、三彩及少量的酱釉、黄瓷、绿瓷等。青瓷出土量较大，有的胎质较差，杂质较多，釉呈豆青色，多杂黑斑点，外壁露胎，釉向下流淌；多数青瓷胎较纯，胎中泛青灰色，釉薄而亮。白瓷多泛青，胎土泛黄，较杂，釉面有冰裂纹现象。个别白瓷胎质白净，上施化妆土，瓷器烧造火候高。黑瓷釉面较薄，略显红褐色。三彩仅见两件。黄彩和绿彩瓷器较少，胎质较松软，釉面有冰裂纹。

器型有碗、罐、钵、瓶等。碗的底部特征差别较大，有大饼状厚足、小饼状足，有的底心上凹。存在少量的玉璧形足，足呈环形璧状，底心内抠，有的呈乳状高凸。仅发现两件圈足白瓷，胎质白净，烧造火候高。酱釉圈足瓷器，内底多有涩圈。绿釉、黄釉瓷器发现较少，仅见壶残片。

出土的陶器可以分为两类：A类为泥质黄褐陶、青灰陶、红陶的宽折沿盆、碗、钵、甑、敛口牛鼻形系罐、卷沿瓮等。B类为泥质灰陶的窄折沿或卷沿盆、沿面弧曲的桥形耳罐等。

遗址中出土瓷片较多的文化堆积从下向上有：堆积64、堆积70、堆积195、堆积69、堆积68。文化堆积与出土瓷器的器型、釉色相结合并联系其他遗址出土瓷器特点，可以将发现瓷器的特点与时代归结如下：

堆积64中，以青瓷为主，所出青瓷分为两大类：A类，豆青色釉，色泽浓绿，杂黑斑点，外壁有流釉现象，其胎土较杂。器型厚重，流行饼形足，内底有三支钉痕。器型有碗、壶等。为北齐时期遗物。B类，胎质青灰，部分罐的外壁呈红褐色，釉色呈青灰色，釉较薄，釉面光亮。流行饼形足，底心上凹，器型较为轻薄。为唐代遗物。堆积中还出有较多的黑瓷片、三彩瓷豆柄。因此，堆积64所出的瓷片时代较为复杂，可能反映了建筑址使用的时间较长。

堆积70中，A类青瓷基本不见，B类青瓷数量较多。出现胎质紧密厚重、色泽光亮开片的青瓷，仅见1块，不同于前者。黑瓷占有一定数量。白瓷仅见1片。出现1件玉璧底。时代为唐代晚期。

堆积69，以白瓷为主，白瓷釉中泛黄、青灰，釉面有冰裂纹，内底有三支钉痕。青瓷数量较少。

堆积68，以白瓷为主，堆积69的白瓷继续存在，出现两件胎质白净、烧造火候高的瓷碗。陶器以泥质灰陶为主，器型有窄折沿或卷沿的盆、沿面弧曲的桥形耳罐。

堆积19、21、5，出土标本较少，有白瓷、酱釉瓷、黄绿彩瓷，器形流行圈足器，酱釉罐、碗内底涩圈。

据此，将遗址发现的陶瓷器分为四大期，第一期：堆积64中的A组青瓷、红褐陶饼状足的钵、碗等，时代为北齐；第二期：堆积64B组、70、195，时代为唐代；第三期：堆积69、68，为宋代。第四期：堆积21、19、5，金元时期或以后。

瓷器的产地，遗址出土的青瓷、白瓷、黑瓷、酱釉瓷及绿彩黄彩以淄博窑口为主。胎质紧密厚重、色泽光亮开片的青瓷瓶标本应为河南窑产品，胎质青灰细密、釉面薄亮的青瓷（标本70：106）应为南方窑口所产，非淄博窑口生产，反映了遗址上活动的人群存在与远方的交流。

二 文化堆积的形成

1．中心台基北侧

第一个阶段：

建筑基址地面在长时间活动使用中，堆积223的土质较细，堆积64和堆积70多瓦、瓦当、砖、瓷片。堆积70北侧厚0.52、南侧厚0.12米，由北向南倾斜。内含大量的陶瓷片瓦片瓦当，时代有北朝、唐早期、唐晚期。应是唐代后期的堆积。

堆积195分布在南侧台基的北侧中部偏西及西侧的北部，堆积中含有较多的瓦片、瓷片、白灰，为南侧台基向北倒塌堆积。标本有唐代黑瓷壶、白瓷碗及较早的青瓷碗等，时代应为唐代晚期。这时南侧台基上的建筑已经倒塌毁坏。

第二个阶段：

堆积69号，较厚的活动面，层面上有烧土面堆积164层面上有一片烧土面，厚五六厘米。该层面上有许多石灰墙皮、大片的。在这层面上应该有较长时间的活动。内存在玉璧底碗底一块。北宋早期的活动遗迹。

第三次活动使用，堆积68，地面平烧灶121、122。内出淄博窑口纯白瓷，圈足。宋代标本。东北部的弧形石墙堆积22、出有造像碎块，残铁器、瓷片等。质量很好的2件白瓷碗应是北宋晚期的标本。是长时期用的活动面。

第三个阶段：

堆积5和4较疏松的灰褐色粉沙土。距地表深0.18～0.42、厚0～0.23米。内中出有大量的瓷片、陶片及少量的瓦当。分布在发掘区中部台地的北半部。应为北宋晚期堆积。

堆积4为近现代文化侧层。大面积分布，堆积较厚，长时间形成。内含青花瓷片、酱釉圈足碗、砖、瓦。烧土颗粒。为近现代文化层（明代或更晚）。

堆积1，现代耕土层。分布整个遗址，为现代耕作活动翻动形成。

2．中心台基南侧

中心台基南侧砖墙南，地面平整，没有发现活动面痕迹。

在东西1063.6米处由台基的南侧砖墙向南砌筑南北向砖墙，残存南北0.8米，仅剩四层砖。上部向西倾斜。为台基使用时修筑的。

台基南侧中部分布堆积188，中部较高，向西倾斜。灰褐色粉沙土，土质较为紧密，土中包含物较少，含少量瓦片、石灰颗粒。厚0.5米。

在堆积188上面垒砌两条南北向砖墙，破坏严重。东侧砖墙堆积165：分布在东西向1058米处，底铺石头，上部南北向顺砌单砖墙体，墙体南北长0.88、残存高0.40米。砖墙向西侧倾斜。西侧砖墙堆积166：分布在东西向1054.6米处。底铺石头，上部南北向顺砌单砖墙体，南北长0.90、残高0.30米。砖墙向东倾斜。两道砖墙东西宽3.52米，二者皆向内侧倾斜，应为一组设施。砖墙与北侧台基对应，分布在台基的正中，可能为台基南侧通道的两面护坡。其内有堆积186和187，包含物较少，共同构成通道。其做法可能是垫筑内侧堆积，包砌两侧护坡形成通道。

石墙堆积74，分布在东西向1050.8米处。用长条形石板垒砌而成，南北长2.9、残高1.06米。石墙上部向东倾斜。其东侧垫土较乱，内中包含大量的瓦片、陶片、瓷片、白灰土等，是用建筑废弃堆积填塞的。应为北部台上建筑废弃后建造的。

石墙堆积73，分布在东西向1053.7米处，保存较长。底部铺石头，其上南北向长条形石板垒砌而成。长1.92、残高0.50米上部向东倾斜。是在晚于石墙74的堆积175、176内挖槽建造的，该道石墙应晚于西侧的石墙堆积74。性质与做法有待分析。

在石墙74的西侧大面积分布着很厚的堆积，有堆积174、178～181，由东向西倾斜，为北侧高地上清理丢弃下来的垃圾土。应为台基顶上清理的时代。堆积178中出有玉璧底白瓷碗底，时代为宋代（晚唐）。堆积181出有牛牙、骨头、蚌壳，这时期遗址上应该存在人类活动。

堆积167，疏松的灰褐土，包含物较之下部堆积明显减少。

堆积178、174形成后，与北侧形成高平台地。后期的人们为了用砖，起取南侧砖墙，形成的0.80米沟槽，在沟槽内丢弃造像残块及其他的遗物，形成堆积15。起取砖的时间早于堆积4和堆积54。

堆积54，为疏松的黄褐沙土，内含少量的陶片和石块。间隔原堆积15与北侧探方内的堆积4相对应，应为同一堆积。时代为金代或以后堆积。

堆积1为耕土层，分布在54的上面。

由于台基的存在，南北堆积联系分析存在困难。在台基的北侧，瓦片大量的存在有两个大的时期：堆积64和70，堆积69和68。台基南侧基本也有两个阶段：74东侧与堆积66间的填塞堆积，74西侧丢弃垃圾堆积。

分析：砖墙165和166间通道使用时，北侧建筑还存在。在北侧建筑遭到比较严重的破坏，形成堆积64和70后，人们向西扩建通道，修筑堆积74，在其内侧填塞建筑垃圾土。这个时段应该是堆积69的人们形成的。堆积74西侧的堆积181是通道使用时形成的堆积。其上的垃圾土应该是堆积

69和68活动较长时间内形成的堆积。

第一阶段：堆积188和砖墙165和166通道使用时；第二个阶段：石墙74东堆积和175、176和181；第三段：174和167、178、179、180、堆积15。

第八章　结语

一　建筑基址

发掘中发现一个长方形的建筑台基，周围有排水院子，下雨的时候可以通过排水口排泄出去。这个做排水用的院子是必须的，发掘期间两次暴雨存满庭院就是证明。台基和院子的边是用砖垒砌的，砖有标准化的盖的，砖的质量不一样，最好的砖在台基南侧用，是加水打磨光滑的。砖间缝隙很小。其他砖墙，质量不好，砖没有特意加工。从南侧来人首先看到南侧主要建筑，

砖墙的主要功能是保护台基的，多为单砖厚度，只有南墙是双砖的厚度。没有采用三合土。

台基上的建筑没有发现什么痕迹，只可以按照院子里的情况（结构与堆积）进行分析：按照院子里瓦的情况，可以确定存在大型瓦顶建筑。建筑顶部用板瓦和筒瓦做成。筒瓦呈长条形凸起。房檐的筒瓦有瓦当。

因为瓦没有发现楔形瓦或条形瓦，因此推测顶部应该是直墙硬山两面坡瓦顶。

瓦当多是A、B型，我们统计比较完整或多半的瓦当，A型共42件、B型76件。可能是两个不同类型建筑的瓦当。据此推测顶部的长度，两个瓦当间的距离应该是42厘米，A型可以复原17.6米的顶部，而B型的可以复原32米的长度。因此，这里存在的是两个大型的建筑。

C～F型瓦当每次仅发现一二个，很惊人的，EF做法很特殊，DEF的大小和一般的瓦当不一样，不应该是上面两个建筑的瓦当。但是由于每次发现较少，也没法说是其他建筑的瓦当。看来，特殊的瓦当应该是从其他遗址的建筑带来的。另一种可能，是当地工作制作瓦当的参考标本。

A、C，图案和明道寺的接近，我们知道当地的工匠知道明道寺的情况。有几个瓦当有红色颜色，这里发现的许多白灰上面饰有红颜色，因此，建筑经过施彩装饰，应该富丽堂皇非常壮观。

建筑用传统的木构，发现的圆帽铁钉说明在建筑的门窗上有此类装饰。而顶部也用大铁钉加固。

西北部的小房子，前侧用木柱支撑、无墙体，地面发现烧烤痕迹，应为烧炊用的服务场所，不是大型宫殿类建筑。

两个情况显示，除了中间建筑外，还有其他大型建筑。在早期堆积发现两种类型的瓦当，因为堆积64包括70A、70B，说明两个建筑在不同的时间倒塌了。另外，堆积70的瓦片堆积厚、大面积分布，而且部分搭盖在北侧的砖墙上，因此，堆积70中的瓦是从北侧高台上倒塌下来的，说明

北侧高台上应该存在瓦顶建筑。在北侧高台的北面没有发现排水保护设施，建筑倒塌毁坏后，上面的地面可能改变较大。

使用佛寺的时候在南墙的中部修筑有通道，用砖垒砌两侧护坡，中间填塞堆积。在建筑东北27米处存在两座陶窑。半成品的石造像说明当地应该存在造像加工作坊。

但是没有外侧围墙及进入寺院的山门。

寺院毁坏的时间在唐代中晚期，佛像砸毁、建筑倒塌。后来又多次使用台基，在台基的南侧加宽修筑通道。但是没有发现晚期的大型瓦顶建筑。宋代后，有人把收藏的残块埋藏在起砖形成的深槽里及南侧的山沟小河边。

二　佛教造像

白龙寺遗址发现了200余件石头造像残块和9件陶塑像残块。在发掘工作开始之前，村民在河边修路时发现了几十件造像残块，其中的26件被临朐县博物馆和考古发掘队收藏。这里对发现的造像和塑像从以下几个方面进行分析。

1．造像材料

石头造像大多选用当地存在的石灰岩石雕刻，所用石材硬度较低，可以用钢铁刀具轻松加工。个别的石头呈黄色或褐色层次分布。选用石材与周邻遗址有相似之处，如青州龙兴寺、兴国寺，临朐明道寺等遗址。

标本TG304-15：16是用砂岩制作的。

2件小的背屏造像是用绿泥石片岩制作，石中含有白云母、磁铁矿和石榴石，这种石头在当地存在。两件小的背屏造像，无论从材质、大小、造像风格以及铭文较为普通的书法水平都与临朐东部的明道寺发现造像相似，可能从明道寺流传过来（明道寺）。标本TG414-BK：4是用滑石做成的，石质地松软。

2．雕刻技法

发现造像都是用一块整石雕刻而成，底座单独制作。造像底部有榫插立在底座卯孔内。造像雕刻技术熟练，刀法自然流畅，表面打磨光滑，局部精雕细刻，纹饰细腻优美。雕刻技术有两种刀法：早期造像用平直刀法雕刻，用一次性刀法刻成，衣服纹饰高凸清晰，菱角分明。衣纹表面平滑是用刀具多次加工而成的。后期造像，表面加工光滑，应用刀具多次雕刻加工形成。有几件造像表面残存彩绘颜色或贴金的痕迹。多数造像加工细致，造型优美，反映了极高的艺术水准。

3．陶塑像

该遗址发现数件陶塑像，其中2件菩萨塑像和底座是用白陶制作，把白陶泥添加在模子里用手按捺成形，烧制而成。白陶塑像较为松软，烧制火候较低。塑像的表面原来可能绘有彩色颜色。在博兴龙华寺和临朐县内发现同样塑像。国外博物馆也有收藏。2件灰陶塑像用泥土捏塑并烧制而成，材料和制法与遗址发现的砖瓦相似，可能是在遗址东北侧的陶窑里烧成的。其风格独特，形体表现浑厚，时代略晚，可能为唐代塑像。

4．造像尺寸

发现的造像大小不一，有的形体高大，如同真人，有的形体矮小，高仅数厘米。标本C：115、15：4应该参照人体原来尺寸制作的。从发现造像尺寸分析，无法确定寺院的主体造像。

5．造像数量

造像多数破损严重，很少个体能够拼对，寺院佛像多数无存。发现的多为造像碎小残块，无法推知造像原来大小。根据发现的有身体的造像或身体残块分析，身体共5个，其中一个塑像与底座一体。从底座部分看，共发现13件石头底座、1件泥质灰陶底座、2件白陶底座，遗址最少应有16件造像或塑像。由于发现残块数量较多，应该存在近百件造像或塑像。

6．造像风格

白龙寺的造像风格可以清楚地看出早晚不同的发展阶段，早期虽然也有薄的衣服，但衣服层数多，衣纹清晰，衣角的表现较为硬朗，不像后期感觉那么薄透。裙角外展，与高大的身体相结合，给人以高大魁梧的感觉。造像面带微笑，和蔼可亲。双眼轻轻的注视着你，似与参拜者相视而语，温和的进行语言沟通、感情交流。晚期的造像有非常薄的衣服，紧紧的贴在身体上，造像身体隐约可见，似有接触到佛或菩萨肉体的感觉。衣服的边角与衣纹相似，裙角瘦紧，贴裹在身体上，造型更为苗条迷人。眼睛微眯，眼神向下斜视，似在思考，似在静修，给人清心淡漠、超然脱世的感觉。艺术风格在较短的时期发生了很大变化，和山东地区其他寺院一样有着共同的发展演变规律。

白龙寺遗址佛教造像镂孔透雕的风格有着独自的特点，标本TG304-15：62、TG304-15：98、C：111、C：126应为镂孔背光，标本C：110为背屏造像残块也为镂空而成。这种复杂的雕刻手法在山东地区其他寺院遗址少见。

7．造像年代

遗址中发现2件有铭文的年代记载，一件有北魏普泰二年（公元532年），"张机张昌兄弟二人"造像底座有"大齐天统四年（公元568年）"。现存临朐博物馆的采集造像中有3件带铭文残块，一件背屏造像有"大魏孝昌……（公元525～527年）"，一件为头光造像残块有"兴和二年（公元540年）"的铭文，一件方形莲座上有"武平七年（公元576年）"的铭文。

从造像所表现的衣服纹饰、身体表现及雕刻技法看，在发现的200余件造像残块中，有19件能够确定为北魏末年到东魏时期（公元525~550年），14件能够确定为北齐时期造像（公元550~577年）。除了1件泥质灰陶佛像可能为唐代，应该没有隋代以后造像。

8. 造像所反映的保藏情况

造像都遭到严重破坏，最大的残块有30厘米之高，多数为较小的残块。因为有的造像个体厚达20余厘米，在破坏的时候用很大的力量或较大的工具并多次敲打才能毁坏。仅发现少量的佛或菩萨头，全部造像的头皆被敲掉，面部特征遭到毁损。

2件背屏头光造像，背面有开凿沟槽修理痕迹，应为破坏后修复使用。没有发现其他修复迹象。

造像表面彩绘颜色与贴金所剩无几，多数造像表面风化严重，仅有一块的打磨光滑部分保存如初。破坏部分一样风化厉害。这显示，造像遭到破坏后，在露天空间里存在较长时间。标本C∶3破坏一面风化严重，而打磨光滑的台面和脚部保存很好，这块造像的台面和脚部应该扣放在地下，而破坏部分暴露在空气里，经历了很长时间被其他堆积覆盖。最早的造像残块是在堆积里发现的，另外一些在其上的堆积里发现，而大量的造像残块是在晚期的灰坑或台基南侧、河边倾斜堆积里发现。

根据前文的分析，白龙寺造像有以下特点：

第一，其用材、制作方法以及造像所反映的艺术风格一脉相承，多为当地工匠用当地所产石材雕刻而成。标本BK∶4为半成品，没有完成雕刻，因此当地应该有雕刻造像的作坊。

第二，所发现的造像大多在较短的时间内制作完成，与青州龙兴寺、临朐明道寺的情况基本一致，在龙兴寺发现的320件佛像中仅有几件晚于北朝。北魏末年至北齐五六十年的时间，在山东地区盛行造像之风，发现大量的佛教造像。

第三，遗址中发现造像和塑像数量较大，有石头雕刻造像、白陶或灰陶塑像，大小不一，造像表面打磨光滑、雕刻精细、造型优美。可以清晰看到从北魏到北齐末年，雕刻技法与艺术风格的延续发展。和其他寺院遗址的情况一样。白龙寺的位置在偏远的深山沟里，却表现出如同青州、临朐、博兴等州府城邑一样的高超水平。 白龙寺的造像反映出其规格较青州显得形体较小。

第四，仅在两件造像残块上发现修理痕迹，而青州龙兴寺的造像大多经过多次修理，反映其造像使用时间较长，应该长达500年之久。在白龙寺多数没有修理的痕迹，其使用时间应该较短。

第五，造像破坏严重，手、头、腿都被砸掉，身体也多被砸成数段，造像遭受了多次严重毁坏。由此可以看出，造像的毁坏是人为故意破坏（强烈活动）而成，不是地震、大水等自然因素或无意的事故形成。

第六，造像的残块是不完整的，多数个体仅保存少量残块。造像残块四下分散丢弃，仅有一个部分是破坏后放在一个灰坑内。这与青州龙兴寺、临朐明道寺故意挖窖穴掩埋不同。

第七，造像的表面大多风化严重，表面镏金或彩绘颜色保存较差，破坏的造像残块长期暴露在露天里风化而成，因为破坏的表面分化也非常厉害，造像破坏后被埋藏的时间较长，可能多达一二百年。

第八，佛像破坏后，寺院建筑大概也毁坏了，僧人离寺它去。如果存在寺院延续使用，还有僧人在这里活动，他们可能把残损的造像残块，继续摆放供奉膜拜。因为，发现造像的最早堆积70，造像破坏的时间可能与堆积70相同。

综上所述，白龙寺遗址六世纪的造像及寺院是在短时间内被被人为毁坏的，应为大型的或有组织的毁佛活动所致，可能与历史上大规模的毁佛活动有关。而造像、寺院破坏后，这里在很长的时间内没有进行与佛教相关的活动。数百年后，有人把造像残块清理、挖坑埋藏。

三　结语

南北朝时期，山东大致经历了刘宋、北魏、东魏和北齐四个时代。

山东北朝时期，社会动荡，征战连年，政权频迭，长期处于分裂混乱之中。在这样一个特定的历史时期和社会环境中，南北文化、胡汉文化、中外文化之间，彼此碰撞，相互交融、构成了北朝时期文化的总体特征。

山东北朝时期道教和佛教并立，给战乱中处于水深火热之中的百姓以精神寄托。山东是道教发源地之一，泰山和崂山一带则为道教活动中心。泰山岱庙和崂山太清宫大约始建于汉代，经历历代修葺，保存至今。

山东北朝佛教艺术遗存可分为佛教寺院、石窟寺、摩崖刻经和佛教造像等四类（图八一）。这时期的佛教寺院大部已毁，现存始建于北朝的寺院有：济南长清灵岩寺和柳埠神通寺、青岛崂山法海寺、枣庄云谷山灵泉保寿禅院、济宁铁塔寺（崇觉寺）、莒县浮来山定林寺、泰山普照寺等。出土佛教造像、刻经碑等佛教遗存的重要佛寺有：青州龙兴寺和兴国寺、临朐明道寺和白龙寺、临淄金陵寺、博兴龙华寺和乡义寺、广饶永宁寺、曲阜胜果寺、鄄城义城寺等。而青州龙兴寺、博兴龙华寺、临朐明道寺和白龙寺等经过考古专业人员发掘和清理，影响较大。石窟寺有济南黄石崖和龙洞、长清莲花洞、东平司里山和青州驼山。摩崖刻经分布于济南、泰山至峄山之间，主要有济南龙洞佛峪、泰山经石峪、新泰徂徕山映像岩、汶上水牛山、东平大洪顶和司里山、邹城四山（铁山、钢山、葛山、尖山）和峄山、滕州陶山等（图八二）。佛教造像、造像碑发现40余处，以青州、博兴、诸城、临朐、临淄和广饶较为集中。青州龙兴寺佛教窖藏计有佛头144件、菩萨头46件、带头残像36件、其他头像10件、造像残躯200余件。造像材料分为石灰石、汉白玉、花岗岩、陶、铁、彩绘泥塑和木等七种质地。造像多有贴金，部分造像彩绘有佛教故事。博兴龙华寺遗址1983年出土北魏至隋代铜造像100余件，其中有铭文44件，有确切纪年的39件。

临朐佛教文化有着悠久的历史，佛教遗存丰富，据明嘉靖三十一年（公元1552年）《嘉靖临

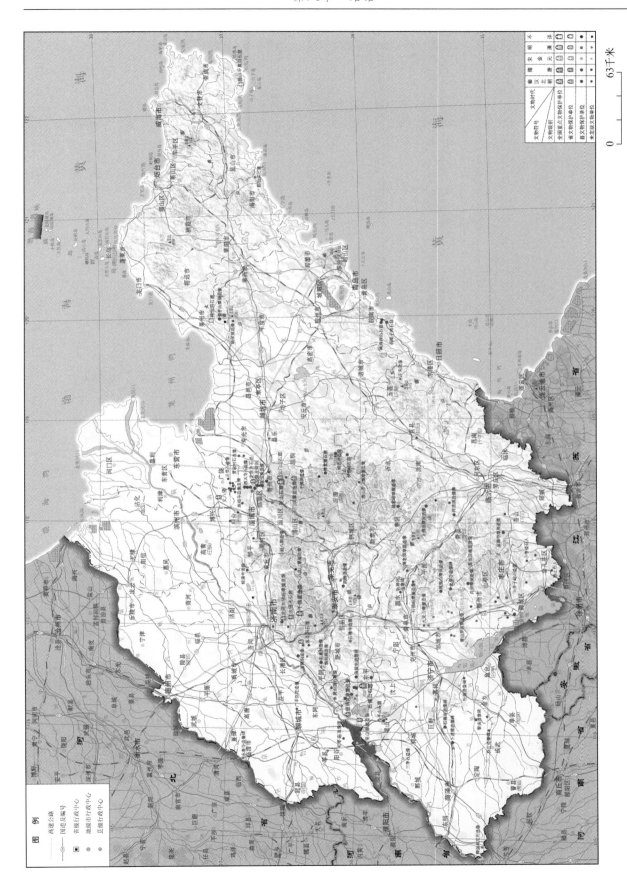

图八一（fig. 81） 山东省石窟寺、石造像及造像碑分布图

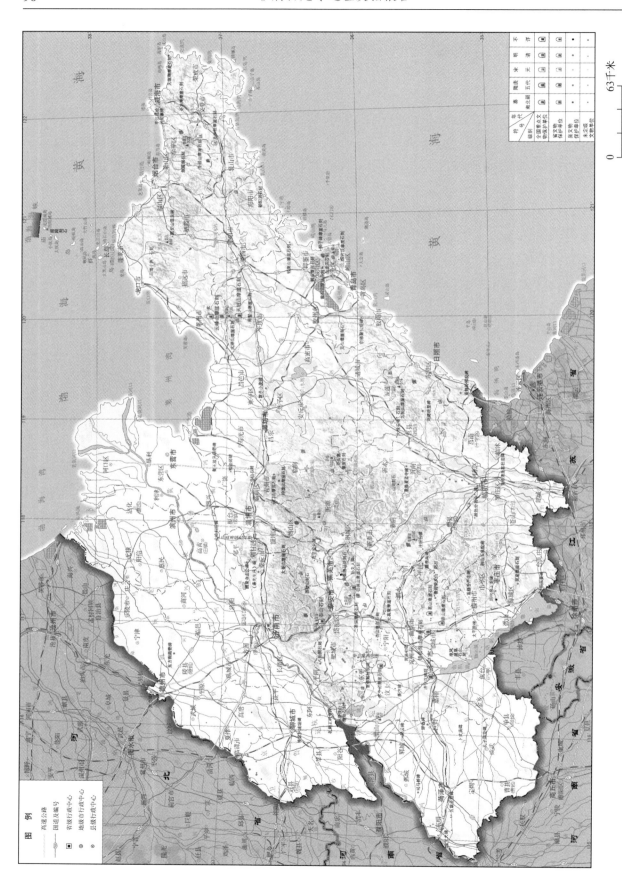

图八二（fig.82）　山东摩崖石刻碑分布图

胸县志》载有34个寺观；清康熙十一年（公元1672年）《康熙临朐县志》载有60个寺观；清光绪八年（公元1882年）《光绪临朐县志》载有祠宇有19处。临朐县现存有大量的佛教寺院、佛教造像、石窟寺和摩崖石刻等佛教遗存，主要有崇圣人僧人墓、重修三元庙碑、老崖崮磨崖刻石、神堂崮石窟、仙姑庙遗址、明道寺、歪头崮摩崖石刻、东镇庙、石佛堂石佛、铸剑池石刻、佛顶尊胜经幢、石门坊摩崖造像、太平崮古建、悬泉寺等等。1984年发掘清理的上寺院明道寺舍利塔地宫出土的千余块北朝晚期至隋代造像，其精美的雕塑艺术手法，独特的风格，众多的纪年造像引人注目。

白龙寺遗址的发掘，清理发掘了一套北朝至隋唐时期山间小型佛教寺院建筑基址。虽然遗址面积较小，建筑址遭到破坏，但是建筑基址全面的揭露发掘，为北朝至隋唐佛教考古以及寺院建筑遗址的研究提供了一套科学完整的资料。佛寺的布局、建造、使用和废弃年代的探讨，遗址文化堆积、埋藏过程的分析，佛像制作、供奉、时代的研究，佛寺与造像毁灭原因的推论为中国佛教考古提供了一个典型案例。

北魏晚期到东魏时期，佛教信徒来到沂山西北、弥河西岸东西长的深山沟里，选择山沟尽头小河北侧的山前向阳台地建造寺院居住修行。这里山高谷深，流水潺潺，丛林茂密，鸟语花香，适宜佛教信徒潜心清修。他们首先将建筑进行了规划布局，把台地平整修理，在中心部位修整一个东西长方形台基，台基的南侧借助断崖，其余三面下挖，并形成围绕台基的凹字形下陷的庭院。台基四周用砖包砌。在中心台基的东西两侧近南面断崖处修建有东西长的慢道与寺院其他建筑沟通，慢道下面砌筑有暗的排水沟将凹字形下陷庭院的水排出。南侧砌筑砖墙，墙上砌筑有排水孔。下陷庭院的西、北、东三面将断面修整，并用砖垒砌形成高台。西侧高台东西宽仅0.90米，但保存较好，顶面用砖平铺，东侧高台结构应该与之相同。北侧高台较高，台地南北宽8.00米，台北挖有一条东西向的深沟向遗址东南延伸，将山坡来水泄掉以形成对佛寺的保护。中心台基的南侧有上下通道。在西侧高台的西北修建有一坐北向南烧炊用的小房子。

从发掘迹象看，中心长方形台基和北侧高台上面的建筑破坏殆尽，没有发现与建筑有关的柱础、墙体等。但由北侧凹陷庭院内堆积70中发现的从北侧高台上倾斜下来大面积成片的瓦和堆积195中发现的从中心台基向北侧倾斜下来的白灰墙体及瓦片分析，中心台基和北侧高台上都有瓦顶建筑，应该皆为坐北向南的建筑。在出土瓦类构件中没有发现歇山顶建筑用的长条瓦条，可能为两面坡硬山瓦顶建筑。倒塌堆积中少见砖，墙体应该是土坯墙，外表涂抹有白灰，上面施红彩。有的瓦当上面绘有红彩，檐下瓦当部分施红彩。房屋的门框可能为石块垒砌，门上饰有大的带圆钉泡的铁钉。两座瓦顶建筑的性质，北侧高台地东西长约28、南北宽8米，台上的建筑应该小到中型的瓦顶建筑。中心台基东西20、南北15米，如果是东西长的殿堂，应该为小型的瓦顶建筑，东西两侧各留二、三米的空间。由堆积70和堆积195分析，在唐代中晚期，北侧高台上的瓦顶建筑先倒塌废弃，过了一段时间，南侧中心台基上的瓦顶建筑也倒塌废弃。其后，这里再没有建造其他的佛寺建筑。

关于院墙和山门，在遗址发掘时作为工作重点进行思考和寻找，有目的的进行了考古勘探和探沟试掘，在现建筑址的外围没有发现院墙，也没有发现山门迹象。

由遗址东北角发现的两座砖窑看，佛寺的修建是就地取材，烧制砖瓦建造而成的。

作为佛寺遗址，供奉数量较多的佛教造像。以石头造像为主，有佛像、菩萨像、造像底座等。造像题记与造像风格分析，造像有北魏晚期、东魏、北齐时期造像。造像大部分内容比较简单，为百姓使用，但个别的造像较为复杂，资助的人应该有较为高深的文化底蕴。由遗址出土的造像半成品看，造像多为当地制作，少量为外地传入。白陶菩萨像和底座应为北齐时期的作品，用瓷土做胎烧制而成，应为淄博一带瓷窑生产的，这类塑像在博兴龙华寺有较多的发现。灰陶塑像应为当地烧造的，其时代为唐代。没有发现隋唐时期的石造像。佛造像的毁灭为彻底的摧毁，把造像砸为较小的残块。由造像表面严重的风蚀情况看，造像破坏后，在寺院地面保存了较长的时间，到了宋代，人们集中处理，掩埋在中心台基南侧砖墙取走后形成的砖墙基槽内，还有较多的造像丢弃在小河边。

寺院与造像的毁灭应为大规模的人为毁坏，是同时期毁灭的。我国历史上有着几次大的灭佛运动，俗称"三武一宗灭佛"，即魏太武帝、北周武帝、唐武宗和后周武宗灭佛。由堆积70和堆积195分析，白龙寺寺院与佛像毁灭的时间在唐代中晚期，而这与唐武宗的"会昌法难"的时间相吻合。唐武宗即位后，开始了对佛教的整顿，各种社会现象加强了他灭佛的决心。唐武宗灭佛，始于会昌初年，而至会昌末年达到高潮。会昌四年（公元844年）裁并天下佛寺，天下各地上州留寺一所，若是寺院破落不堪，便一律废毁；下州寺院全部拆废。天下一共拆除寺庙4600余所，僧尼26万余人还俗成为国家的两税户，没收寺院所拥有的膏腴上田数千万顷，没收奴婢为两税户15万人。会昌法难可能波及影响到深山沟里的白龙寺，佛像被砸毁，寺院遭到了彻底的毁灭。也可能有其他原因，不得而知。

寺院毁灭后，在宋代时候这里有人群在活动。他们在中心台基南侧砖墙前，修建上下通道，在中心台基的西侧挖坑烧炊，这里可能还存在围绕中心台基的活动。

遗址的发掘，给了我们许多新的发现，为佛教考古的研究提供了新的线索。但是面对残毁的佛像，再看砖瓦断墙，还有一些问题三思而不得其解。

发现的造像残块大概属于一百个个体，原来的使用佛像可能更多，为什么这么小的寺院需要这么多的佛像，在这狭小的空间里又是怎样摆放陈列的？

佛像多为北朝晚期制作的，只有一件隋唐佛像时期的塑像时代较晚，说明佛寺主要活动特别是资助制作佛像是在北朝晚期进行的，隋唐时期基本没有佛像的制作活动。瓷器标本及文化堆积反映，造像与佛寺的毁灭在唐代晚期。那么隋唐时期为什么只用前代的佛像供奉，这时期的僧人和供养人为什么不资助或制作佛像？这种情况在附近的大寺院如青州龙兴寺等地也存在。为什么形成这种现象？有待今后工作的深入研究。

白龙寺遗址开始调查勘探并立项进行合作发掘时，关于佛寺遗址科学的考古发掘和研究工作进行的还较少。我们期望遗址的发掘、报告的出版，能为学界提供科学翔实的资料，推动佛教考古的进一步发展。

The Site of the White Dragon Temple in Linqu, Shandong

The report on the excavation of the Temple of the White Dragon was assembled in Chinese language. This English version is an abridged translation that was added to make the book accessible to an international audience. The authors joined some sections and condensed some content that seemed to be of interest to a specialist Chinese speaking public only but aimed to include all crucial information. For quotations and all referencing purposes the reader is kindly requested to turn to the Chinese original.

1. Introduction

Shandong Province is located in eastern China, along the lower reaches of the Yellow River. It borders the Bohai Sea and the Huanghai Sea in the east (fig. 1). The landscape of Shandong is varied. The centre of the province is mountainous and has the highest terrain. The east and south of the province is hilly and the north and west consists of plains. The highest mountains are Mount Tai 泰山 reaching to 1,532 meters, Mount Lu 鲁山 with 1,108 meters and Mount Yi 沂山 with 1,031 meters above sea level. The main rivers Zi 淄, Mi 弥 and Wei 潍 flow north to enter the Bohai Sea. The Buddhist site of Xiao Shijiazhuang 小时家庄 Village is located in the valley between Mount Lu and Mount Yi.

Linqu county lies in the central part of Shangdong Province. It borders Qingzhou 青州 county in the north, Yishui 沂水 and Yiyuan 沂源 counties in the south, Zibo 淄博 county in the west, and Changle 昌乐 and Anqiu 安丘 counties in the east (fig. 81). Central and southern Linqu is hilly whereas the north is relatively plain.

The principle water sources flowing through Linqu are the Mi 弥 and the Wen 汶 rivers and their tributaries. The Mi river originates in the Tianqi Bay 天齐湾 at the foot of mount Yi, meanders west along the mountain slope, bends northeast near the town Jiushan 九山, passes through the Yeyuan 冶源 reservoir and Qingzhou, and later branches into several streams before it reaches the Bohai Sea.

Linqu has a semi humid temperate climate with cold and dry winters and hot and humid summers. The average temperature is $-3\,^{\circ}\text{C}$ for January and $25–26\,^{\circ}\text{C}$ for July.

The name Linqu 临朐 can be traced back to the Western Han period (206 BC–9 AD). During the period under discussion here, the 6th to 9th centuries, the county assumed various names. Under the Northern Wei dynasty (386–534) Linqu belonged to Jiaozhou 胶州 Prefecture and was called Zhuxu 朱

虚. Under the Northern Qi (550–577) and the succeeding Northern Zhou (557–581) it was part of Langya 琅琊 Prefecture and was called Changguo 昌国. In the Sui (581–618) and Tang (618–907) Dynasties, it was called Linqu and belonged to Beihai 北海 Prefecture. In later periods it was mostly affiliated with Qingzhou and was called Linqu. Today Linqu belongs to the administrative unit Weifang City 潍坊市.

The temple site of Xiao Shijiazhuang lies at the foot of a hill near Da Shijiazhuang 大时家庄, a village that is located in the north-western part of Shijiahe 石家河 township in Linqu county. The site is about 30 km south of Linqu county town. Its coordinates are 118°28'05.1″ E and 36°15'15.5″ N, and its altitude is 258 m above sea level (fig. 2, pls. 1 .1–2).

If one starts off from Shijiahe township and follows the west bank of the Mi River, then from Dagudong 大崮东 Village proceeds westbound along the bank of a Mi River tributary, and turns north in Xiao Shijiazhuang, one will encounter a valley that suddenly opens up. This place is quite secluded – the valley is surrounded by mountains that open only to the southeast.

East and west of the temple site are ravines which protect the area from flash floods. To the front is the small watercourse which meanders east to join the Mi River. The mountains surrounding the site help blocking the cold winds in winter but the opening on the southeast lets in breezes in summer. The valley receives plenty of sunlight; it is warm in winter and cool in summer. The soil is fertile. From an environmental and geographic viewpoint the valley is very suitable for habitation as well as for establishing a Buddhist temple.

At the outset of the collaboration the team named the site 'White Dragon Temple'. The choice of this name was not unfounded. The *Linqu County Chronicle of the Jiajing period* 嘉靖临朐县志 of 1552 states that "there is a White Dragon Temple 65 li to the south of the county town"; The *Chronicle of Linqu County of the Kangxi period* 康熙临朐县志 of the year 1672 further states that "the White Dragon Temple, also called the Cross Hall, is at Changzhuangshe, 60 li from the county town." The geographical location recorded in the county chronicles closely matches that of the excavation site. Furthermore, there is an old belief among the local population in the White Dragon. To the north of the excavation site there are remains of a castle on a flat hill top. One of its inscriptions mentions a 'White Dragon Shrine' 白龙神庙. To the northeast there is a White Dragon Cave 白龙洞 where architectural remains and stele inscriptions were also discovered, including a well-preserved stele documenting an imperial order granting the establishment of a White Dragon Shrine.

During the actual excavation we found no inscription that would shed light on the original name of the buildings. According to standard archaeological practice the site should be named 'Architectural Remains of the Xiaoshijiazhuang Buddhist Temple' 小时家庄佛寺建筑遗址. However, considering local folklore and the fact that 'White Dragon Temple' had already been used extensively during the application and preparation of the project, we decided to continue naming the site the 'White Dragon Temple' Bailongsi 白龙寺.

This report presents the outcome of the joint Swiss-Chinese investigation and excavation of Bailong Temple site in Xiao Shijiangzhuang, Linqu county. It documents the site and the artefacts in descriptions and in maps, photographs, drawings and ink rubbings, and aims to offer abundant material for the study of Buddhist remains of the Northern Dynasties. It further presents the results of our discussions of the material from the excavation. However, some questions raised by the report still need to be further explored. We look forward to criticism from colleagues and an academic discussion. This report is also the result of the joint application of different approaches, methods and technologies as practised in archaeology in Switzerland and in China. We demonstrate here how we have put a scholarly cooperation into practice together, and hope that this will elicit further discussion.

Finally, we would like to thank the Chinese and Swiss governments and participating experts for many years of ardent attention, support and guidance.

2. Investigation procedure

The excavation site is located in a valley west of Xiao Shijiazhuang, on the slopes of the hill north of the river. The deep loess layers on the hill side had been levelled into terraces already in early historic times and are farmed with corn and winter crops today. The temple site extends over two of the south-facing terraces half-way up the hill (fig. 3, pls. 1; 14; 15).

The area was first surveyed using the Chinese Luoyang Spade (洛阳铲), followed by several probing trenches and one excavation field in 2003. During the second season in 2004 the site was divided into nine fields of 10 m square. To the sides of the main excavation area, the team opened seven additional ditches and unearthed two kilns to the northeast of the main site. The excavation fields (*tanfang* 探方, T) and the trenches (*tangou* 探沟, TG) were then investigated layer by layer. All layers, profiles and finds were mapped in a 3D grid using a total station, and recorded in drawings and photographs (fig. 4, pls. 5–12). After the excavation, the finds, specimen, and the documentation materials were put into the care of the working station of the Institute of Archaeology of Shandong Province in Linzi.

3. Archaeological remains

The temple remains consisted of several areas: a central platform, a wide trench running along its eastern, western and northern sides in the shape of the character "凹" (fig. 16, pls. 14–17), two pathways connecting the central platform with the adjoining terraces to the east and west, two water outlets below the pathways, and the surfaces of the adjoining terraces. In addition we located an entrance situation to the south of the central terrace, and a small building to the northwest of the trench. About 30 meters northeast of the site, two brick kilns came to light.

Central area

The temple was built on a horizon last used during the Warring States period (476–221 BC). The area had been levelled into a terrace, with the terrace borders facing south. The central platform measured 15.4 m north to south and 20 m east to west. Its original surface had been eroded. The remaining height was between 0.8 and 1.2 m (fig. 16, pls. 14–15).

A ditch was dug around the central platform, separating the rectangular central platform from the remaining ground. The ditch had a regular shape, forming a rectangular area in the north with two narrower rectangular extensions to the south. The area in the north extended 27 m east to west and 7 to 7.6 m north to south. The southern extensions were 19 m long and 2.8 to 3 m wide. The ground surface of the ditch was levelled. There were no traces of a walking surface or signs of permanent use (fig. 16, pl. 17). Apparently the main function of the ditch was the protection of the central platform and its buildings from water coming down the steep slopes of the hill to the north.

The borders of the ditch and the south face of the terrace were originally lined with brick walls. The brick walls were half skinned and in some areas single skinned (figs. 18, 19, 23, pls. 16–17). At the northern end of the western border of the ditch, in the height of 90 cm, a small platform extended westwards. The brick-paved platform measured 2.80 m from north to south and was between 70 and 90 cm deep. It was built at the same time as the brick walls of the ditch. The original function of this small platform remains unclear (pls. 15.1 and 25.1).

The southern brick wall of the central platform had extension walls to both sides. They covered the south faces of the connecting pathways with the water outlets. The extension walls turned south in line with the eastern and western borders of the ditch. The southern ends of these walls could not be determined as they were cut off by the modern terrace border (fig. 18, pl. 19.1).

The south side of the central platform was lined with a double-skinned brick wall while the remaining walls east and west of it as well as the walls around the trench were single or half skinned. The walls of the central platform and the wall to the north of the trench recessed from foundations about one brick wide. The foundations were bordered by a row of bricks placed upright into the ground with one corner facing upwards. The east and west walls of the ditch as well as the extension walls covering the water outlets did not show any trace of such ornamental foundation layers (figs. 18,19,23,24, pl. 16–17). The bricks of the south-facing, double-skinned wall of the central terrace were of high quality. Apparently these bricks had been selected carefully for their grey colour without oxidisation spots, their perfectly cuboid shape, and their smooth surface. The remaining walls had bricks of variable quality.

The two pathways that connected the central platform with the adjoining terraces were 4.52 m and 3.8 m wide respectively. Their surface was level with the surfaces of the platforms. Inset into the pathways were water outlets running north-south. They were built with stone and bricks. While only one outlet was found below the western pathway, the eastern water outlet had been built in two stages. The lower outlet was lined with stones in the same way as the western one. Later its southern opening was sealed with bricks and a second brick-lined outlet was added at a higher level (figs. 20,21,22, 26, pls. 19–21).

The surface of the adjoining terrace to the west was even and had a walking horizon. The original surface of the terrace east of the trench was not preserved (pls. 14–15).

Small building

The northern section of the western adjoining terrace revealed the remains of a small building. The ground plan was rectangular, measuring 5.04 by 4.32 m. To the east, north and west it had walls that were 0.6 to 0.9 m wide. The remaining height of the walls was around 0.8 m. These walls were built of a composite of gravel stones, bricks, and clay. On the south side, a flat foundation stone set into the ground about 1.34 m from the western wall indicated that this side had been left open and that the roof was originally supported by two wooden posts. The ground inside the building was even and showed remains of fireplaces and traces of use. Apparently the small stone building was erected when the temple was active (fig. 28, pl. 29).

Kilns

On the terrace to the north of the central platform the surface was eroded. There were no remains of additional platforms or ditches. 27 m to the northeast of the ditch border two kilns were found. Both had been used at the same time and were of comparable size and layout. The western kiln had a brick built firing opening that was 46 cm wide and 30 cm high. The kiln chamber had no brick lining and was dug into the loess terrace. It had a nearly square ground plan with rounded corners in the south, measuring 3.02 by 2.88 m. To the rear the chamber had a raised brick-lined firing platform that was 0.46 m high and 1.1 m deep. The ceiling of the kiln had been supported by a clay post. The ground in front of the kilns was levelled and used as preparation area.

The kilns apparently produced bricks and tiles for the temple. 12 fired bricks were still found on the firing platforms inside the eastern kiln and three more in the western kiln. The kilns were contemporary with the temple (fig. 29, pls. 30–31).

Other remains

To the northeast of the trench a small tomb was found. It was 2.01 m long, 1.15 m wide, with a depth of 1.10 m. It set in below the recent layer 21, with its ground one meter below the current surface. As its irregularly built walls of stone slabs and bricks cut through the remains of the northern ditch wall it can be assumed that it was built long after the temple had perished. The tomb contained two skeletons, one of which had dislocated bones. The tomb contained a ceramic jar and a ceramic lamp which dated to the Ming period (1368–1644). Apparently this was the tomb of a man and a woman of modest social status, one of whom had been reburied (fig. 32, pl. 34).

The layers above the temple horizon revealed further signs of secondary use: several fire places and pits as well as a later stone-built reinforcement of the southern terrace face and an entrance site (figs. 27,30,31, pls. 28, 33).

4. Finds

During the excavation we discovered large amounts of shards of ceramic vessels, ceramic building materials, and fragments of sculptures. The ceramic shards will be discussed in the section "chronology and date". Further to the stone and ceramic objects we found several iron objects (mainly building implements and tools, fig. 57), some personal items such as belt hooks and an ear cleaner made of bronze (fig. 58, pls. 52.1–2), and several bone and horn implements (fig. 59, pl. 53). The site bore only a small number of bronze coins: three *wuzhu* 五铢 coins dating to the Sui dynasty (581–618), one *Kaiyuan tongbao* 开元通宝 (edited from 621), one *Qianyuan zhongbao* 乾元重宝 (edited from 758), and a small coin with indistinct inscription (pls. 52.3–6).

Building materials

Next to four stone fragments that may have formed part of door or window frames the building materials consisted mainly of bricks, roof tiles, ornamental eve plates, and plaster remains.

a) Bricks

The bricks used at the site have a coarse body of grey and in some cases of reddish colour. Mainly one standard size was used. The bricks were between 32 and 34 cm long, 16 cm wide, and 6 cm high. One large face usually showed impressions of straw mats. The other faces were smooth and sometimes polished. One fragment of a brick of different dimensions came to light in layer 70.

b) Tiles

Large amounts of roof tiles and tile fragments were found. While most fragments had to be discarded the team collected and recorded samples of well-preserved tiles, as well as all eve plates *wadang*, i.e. round finishing plates with relief decoration added to the outer end of eve tiles.

Tiles were made in two standardised shapes and sizes: narrow tiles of half-round cross section with a half-tubular extension at one end, and wide, flat, and slightly bent tiles of more or less rectangular shape. All had a coarse grey or dark-grey body.

The narrow tiles were 13 to 15 cm across and 35 to 37 cm long, with a body thickness of 1 cm. The tenons at the end measured about 12 cm in diameter. The outer surface was smooth while the inner surface showed rough cloth impressions. Ca 2 cm from the front end and running parallel to it, they bore an incised recession that was carved out when the clay was still smooth. The edges of the half-tubus were scratched smooth before firing.

The wide tiles were between 34 and 37 cm long and about 2 cm thick. On their front side they were 29 and at the narrower side 25 cm wide. The outer surface was smooth while the inside had rough cloth impressions. The front part was smoothed on the inside and slightly wedge-shaped (figs. 33,34, pl. 35).

c) Eve plates *wadang*

Ornamental end plates were added to narrow eve tiles only. Eve tiles of the wide version displayed no difference to regular tiles. Eve plates were made of the same coarse grey material as the tiles. The ornaments were impressed with moulds.

Six types of decorated eve plates were found at the site.

Type A: The first was impressed with a lotos blossom with eight petals in high relief, eight narrow stamen in-between, and a raised pistil in the centre. Petals and pistil were surrounded by fine lines. The anthers widen towards the outside. The ornament was surrounded by a raised border. Many were carefully executed with the relief showing fine lines and sharp ridges. The reverse was uneven and showed thumb marks. The tile ends had a diameter of 14–14.5 cm. They were joined to the tile when still soft. The joining areas were then smoothed with clay. Of this type, layer 64 contained 10 complete *wadang* (smaller fragments not counted), layer 70 contained 7, and layer 195 contained 3. Altogether 42 complete eve plates of type A were found on the site (fig. 35, pl. 36.1).

In front of the southern wall of the central platform a ceramic fragment with identical decoration came to light in which the relief was recessed instead of raised (15:25). This was apparently the fragment of a mould in which this type of eve plate was made (pl. 36.4).

Type B: The second type displayed a lotos blossom with six petals in relief as well as six wide stamen with large tripartite anthers and a raised pistil. The ornament was surrounded by a raised border. Eve tile plates of this type were executed with less care than the ones of the first type. Often the ornament medallions were not perfectly centred. Others were badly fired at uneven temperature. Many had been burned black. Since the relief had few sharp ridges one can assume that the same moulds had been used for a large number of tiles. The reverse was uneven and showed thumb marks. The tile ends had a diameter of 14–15.5 cm. Most were joined to the tile by attaching it to the front face when still wet. In some instances one section of the border of the end plate was, when still soft, removed with a knife. The plate was then inserted into the inside of an already hardened tile where it was fixed with soft clay and with the help of the incised line observed before. Eve plates of this type were found in layers 64 (1 piece), 70 (34 pieces), 195 (3 pieces), 69 (2 pieces). Altogether 76 more or less complete *wadang* of this type were found (fig. 36, pls. 36.5 and 37.1–2).

Type C: This type was similar to Type A in layout and dimension. Different were the stamen. The filament rose as fine lines with delicate, three-partite anthers. The outlines of petals and pistil were traced with fine lines. The reverse was uneven and showed thumb marks. The joining method was similar to the one of type A. The joining border between tile and end plate was straight and clearly visible. Only two fragments have been found, one in layer 70 and one in layer 68 (T 434, 70.9, and T 433, 68.2). Both were painted in cold pigment after firing with the petals being coloured alternatingly red and white (figs. 37.1–2, pl. 36.6).

Type D: This type showed a lotos blossom with six petals surrounded by fine lines and six stamens. The filament was executed as fine raised lines. The anthers were shown as small squares. The ornament was sharp and finely executed. The reverse was uneven and showed thumb marks. The joining method was similar to the one of type A. The diameter was smaller than the one of the preceding end plates and measures only 13 cm. Only one piece of this type was found (TG1, 5.1, fig. 37.3, pl. 37.7).

Type E: This type showed a lotos blossom with eight petals and stamen. The petals were thin and had no bordering line. The stamens had fine stems and cross-shaped anthers. The raised border was thin and very high. The reverse was flat with a regularly shaped, rounded border. This indicates that this type was made by spreading clay in a plate or flat bowl with high straight borders before impressing the mould plate with the ornament from above. This method differs from the ones used for the preceding examples which were made by impressing clay into an open mould by hand. The diameter was 16.4 cm. The only example of this type was found in layer 178 (T 413, 178.5, fig. 37.4, pl. 37.4).

Type F: This type showed a lotos blossom with eight petals and stamen. The voluminous petals were two-lobed and had slightly raised borders. The reverse was uneven and bore thumb marks. The outside border of the eve plate was uneven and showed raised knobs that fitted into holes on the inside surface of a tile. Apparently in this case the holes were impressed into the body of the tile. When the tile was half dry, a still soft end plate was pressed into the tile and the connections were smoothed with wet clay. This joining method differs from the ones observed before. Type F was larger than the standard eve plates and measured 16 cm in diameter. Two *wadang* of this type were found, one in layer 64 (T 434, 64.1) and one in layer 70 (T 434, 70.17). At the time of excavation the first still bore some traces of red pigment (fig. 38, pl. 37.5).

Buddhist images

At the site of the Temple of the White Dragon more than 200 fragments of stone statues and remains of nine ceramic fig.urines were excavated. In the years preceding the excavation, peasants of the local village had found several dozen additional sculpture fragments. Linqu museum and members of the excavation team managed to secure 26 of these fig.ures.

a) Excavated stone fig.ure fragments

The site contained fragments of sculptures made of stone as well as of white and grey ceramics. At the time of excavation very few sculptures were well preserved. Most had been damaged severely. The fragments originally belonged to images of free-standing Buddha and bodhisattva fig.ures, fig.ure triads with mandorla, and fig.ure stands.

1: TG3-15:17

Fragment of fig.ure stele.

Green chlorite schist, height 15 cm

The fragment is made of green chlorite schist and carved in a rough manner. It has flat cutting surfaces. The fig.ure stele has a conical tenon below that could be placed into a separate stand which has not been preserved. The top section including the fig.ure heads, the left side and a part of the tenon have been broken off.

The fig.ure stele presents a standing Buddha with one hand raised in *abhaya* mudra, the other lowered in *varada* mudra. The Buddha is dressed in a coat of several layers covering both shoulders. The lower hems are flaring out to the sides.

The remaining Bodhisattva is standing upright and is dressed in a heavy suit that covers both shoulders. Long ribbons run crosswise over the body and are held together with a round disk. In its left hand the bodhisattva holds an object which may have been a flask.

The reverse side of the stele is undecorated but retains 10 characters of an incomplete inscription: ...(普) 泰二年」...趙鸞女」...敬造供養。"In the second year of *putai* (532) ... Mrs. Zhao Yangnü ... has this reverently made, with veneration!" (figs. 60.1–3, pls. 54.1–2).

2: TG3-15:13

Fragment of a fig.ure stele

Green chlorite schist, height 12 cm

The fragment is made of a material similar to the stele described above (no. 1, 15.17). The carving displays flat cutting surfaces. Only the feet of a Buddha, its base, the lower hem of the dress, and the tenon are preserved. Originally this object may have been a three-fig.ure stele of slightly larger dimensions than 15.17. The style suggests a dating similar to 15.17, that is the last years of Northern Wei or the early 530s. The undecorated reverse side originally bore a roughly cut inscription. Only the two characters *shi* 世 and *xi* 西 remain legible (figs. 61.1 –2, pls. 54.3 –4).

3: TG202-217:1

Standing Buddha

Limestone, height 21 cm

The surface of this image is severely weathered. It has flat cutting surfaces. The head, most of the mandorla, and the tenon are missing. The fig.ure holds one hand raised in *abhaya* mudra, the other lowered in *varada* mudra. The heavy coat covers both shoulders. Its lower hems flare out to the left and right. Prominent folds of the heavy attire cover the body completely. The reverse side is flat and undecorated. The fragment was part of a fig.ure stele of the late Northern Wei period. It should be one of the earliest images from the White Dragon temple site (fig. 68.2, pls. 60.2–3).

4: TG304-15:56、15

Head of a Bodhisattva

Limestone, height8.2 cm

Two fragments of this limestone object were found. The surfaces on all sides are severely weathered. The cutting method is unclear. Only vague facial features are still visible. The mouth of the fig.ure is smiling. The hair is arranged in three curves above the forehead. The bodhisattva wears a diadem with ribbons hanging down to both sides. The reverse side shows a fragmented extension which indicates that the Bodhisattva was originally connected to a halo or the mandorla of a stele. The image probably dates to the late Northern or Eastern Wei periods（fig. 60.4, pl. 55.1）.

5: TG304-15:69、70

Head of a Bodhisattva

Limestone, height 14.5 cm

The limestone object consists of two fragments. The surface is strongly eroded on all sides but still shows traces of flat cutting surfaces. Several parts of the head are missing, only the lower face and the right part of the head remain. The bodhisattva has full cheeks with a deeply inset mouth which is smiling. Behind the large ear with elongated earlobe a hair band or ribbon is running downwards. The rear of the head was rounded with no indication of a connection to a halo. The head may have belonged to a free-standing fig.ure.

The facial features are comparable to sculptures from Longxing temple and should date to the late Northern Wei or Eastern Wei period（fig. 60.5, pl. 55.2）.

6: TG304-15:35

Upper torso of a Buddha

Limestone, height 26 cm

The fragment is badly damaged. Most of the original surface is lost. Only part of the robe in front and a part of the undecorated back of the object remain. The carving displays flat cutting surfaces. The prominent folds have a hard appearance. The object should be a fragment of a large fig.ure stele. It can be dated to the late Northern or Eastern Wei period（figs. 62.2–3, pl. 55.5）.

7: TG304-15:14

Lower torso of a Buddha

Limestone, height 21 cm

Only the front and the rear of the object retain sections of the original surface. The carving shows flat cutting surfaces. The front shows the multi-layered robe of a standing Buddha with prominent, rhythmic folds and flaring lower hems. The rear part of the object is flat and undecorated. The fragment was apparently part of a large stele. It should date to the late Northern and Eastern Wei periods.

Material and thickness of the fragment as well as the shape and execution of the folds are comparable to the upper torso described above (no. 6, 15.35). It is possible that both were part of the same Buddha image (figs. 62.4–5, pl. 56.1) .

8: TG105-15:73

Torso fragment of a Bodhisattva

Limestone, height 8 cm

The original surface is preserved on the front and rear. It has flat cutting surfaces. The front displays the ornamented attire of a bodhisattva with pearl strings and prominent folds in high relief. Folds are also engraved on the reverse side. The fragment was part of the left leg section of the lower torso of a free-standing Bodhisattva image. It should date to the late Northern or Eastern Wei periods (figs. 64.1–2, pl. 57.1) .

9: TG304-15:34

Lotos stand fragment

Limestone, height 13 cm

The original surface is preserved on the front, left, right and underside. It has flat cutting surfaces. The rear of the lotos stand has been broken off. Originally it may have been connected to a mandorla. The double-lobed lotos petals are facing downwards. Above the lotos there are traces of the round base of a fig.ure. The underside reveals a lotos stem in high relief. The stand should belong to a fig.ure stele of the late Northern or Eastern Wei periods (figs. 64.3–4, pl. 57.2) .

10: TG304-15:24

Fragment of a fig.ure stele

Limestone, 10.5 cm long.

Of this fragment only part of the front and back surfaces still survive. It has flat cutting surfaces. The front shows part of a halo, consisting of a row of radiating bands and five concentric lines. The reverse surface is polished and bears remains of fine line carving which apparently shows the folds and hems of robes. Originally the object was a part of the mandorla of a fig.ure stele that was decorated on both faces. It dates to the late Northern or Eastern Wei periods (figs. 65.4–5, pl. 56.2) .

11: US:1

Fragment of a halo

Limestone, height 5 cm

The front surface of this fragment shows remains of a halo consisting of a row of radiating bands and five concentric lines. The reverse surface is polished but undecorated. The carving shows flat cutting surfaces. The object dates to the Northern or Eastern Wei period.

Since material, thickness and ornamentation of this object are similar to the preceding one (no 10, TG304-15:24) both may originally have belonged to the same stele. The objects were found in different locations: the first next to the southern wall of the central platform, and the latter next to the street by the river （fig. 65.6, pl. 58.3）.

12: TG304-15:53

Base fragment

Limestone, height 22 cm

The fragment retains the two slim feet of a standing image. The tenon is largely preserved. Its surface is roughly cut and not polished. The carving shows flat cutting surfaces. The fragment should date to the late Northern or Eastern Wei periods （fig. 66.3）.

13: T434-195:11

Fig.ure fragment

Limestone, height 6 cm

The fragment shows part of the right arm and hand of a Buddha fig.ure. There are some remains of gilding. The fragment should belong to the late Northern or the Eastern Wei period. （fig. 67.2）

14: TG304-15:81

Torso fragment

Limestone, height 4.5 cm

This fragment shows a part of the torso and the left hand of a standing Buddha. It has flat cutting surfaces. The hand is lowered in the *varada* mudra. The fragment should date to the late Northern or Eastern Wei periods （figs. 67.3–4, pl. 57.5）.

15: TG204-15:79

Hand fragment

Limestone, height 8 cm

The fragment shows the left hand of a Buddha, lowered in *varada* mudra. The arm is covered by an undecorated coat which is running downwards behind the hand. It has flat cutting surfaces. The object should date to the late Northern or Eastern Wei periods （fig. 67.4, pl. 59.2）.

16: TG304-15:28

Hand fragment

Limestone, height 7 cm

The fragment shows the left hand of a bodhisattva. The hand has long, slender fingers which hold the fold of a robe or a stole. The object should date to the late Northern or Eastern Wei periods （fig. 67.5, pl. 59.3）.

17: TG304-52、53:1

Fragment of a Buddha

Limestone, height 30 cm

The fragment of the chest of a Buddha still shows the collar hem of his inner garments engraved as a double line, and some folds of the outer robe running down to the left side of the body. The decoration has flat cutting surfaces. The reverse side is undecorated and flat. Originally the object was part of a large fig.ure stele of the late Northern or Eastern Wei periods (figs. 69.3–4).

18: T414-BK:4

Stone fragment

Talc schist, height 9 cm

The object is of a very soft, greenish material. On several sides it shows traces of carving but it is impossible to say what part of a fig.ure the fragment may belong to. One side shows folds of a robe carved in high relief, possibly of the lower part of a standing Buddha. The folds are, however, not fully executed and finish in sections of unworked stone. Apparently this is an unfinished object. The discovery is significant. As it seems unlikely that half-worked fragments were transported over long distances it suggests that sculptures may have been carved at the site of the temple. According to the style of the folds and the carving method, the object should date to the late Northern Wei or Eastern Wei period （fig. 71.1, pl. 57.6）.

19: TG202-216:1

Fragment of a halo

Limestone, height 16 cm

This is the fragment of a round halo which originally had a diameter of about 46 cm. It has flat cutting surfaces. It shows the torso of a person in high relief standing on a lotos pedestal. The person holds its hands folded in front of his chest. It is dressed in the heavy robe of a monk which covers both shoulders and shows prominent folds. The hems of an inner garment are also visible. Lotos stems and petals cover the background.

The reverse side of the halo is roughly hewn. A wedge-shaped incision indicates that the object was repaired after an earlier damage. The object dates to the Eastern Wei period （fig. 68.1, pl. 60.1）.

20: TG304-15:16

Fragment of a hand

Sand stone, height 14.5 cm

The fig.ure to which this right hand belonged was made of a fine sand stone. The surface is weathered. The carving shows rounded surfaces. The fingers are slightly bent. The inside surface of the hand still retains some traces of red pigments on a white grounding. The arm is covered by an undecorated coat. The fragment should date to the Eastern Wei or early Northern Qi, that is to the 540s and 550s（pl. 55.3）.

21: TG105-15:6

Lower torso of a Buddha

Limestone, height 29.5 cm

Feet and torso of this Buddha image are broken off. The remaining surfaces are weathered, but well preserved. It has flat cutting surfaces. Two layers of robes are visible. The robes of the standing Buddha are soft and reveal the shape of the legs. The reverse side shows the hems of two sets of garments. The image should date to the Northern Qi period（figs. 63.1–2, pls. 56.2–3）.

22: TG304-15:62

Fragment of a *feitian*

Limestone, height 8 cm

Head and arms of the *feitian* are b oken off. The fragmented reverse side still retains part of a background it was attached to. The fragment has rounded cutting surfaces. The left leg of the *feitian* is streched while the right leg is slightly bent. The arms are raised. The background, possibly a halo, shows some traces of carved floral and open-work decoration. The reverse side is slightly rounded and undecorated. The fragment was part of the open-work halo of a fig.ure dating to the Northern Qi period （fig. 65.1, pl. 57.3）.

23: TG304-15:23

Base with two fig.ures

Limestone, height 10 cm, depth 7 cm,

The top and a section of the lower part of the object are broken off. The cuboid object has a flat face on the underside, indicating that it formed the base of a larger image. The front shows two fig.ures in high relief sitting opposite each other in half cross-legged position. The head of the right fig.ure is well preserved. Broad lines indicate that its long hair was combed back. In its right hand the fig.ure holds a small bird. The head of the second fig.ure is damaged. In its raised left hand it holds a round object which may be a human head or skull. The reverse and both side faces are smooth and undecorated. The object may have been made during the Northern Qi period（fig. 65.2, pl. 57.4）.

In discussions of Dunhuang murals paired fig.ures holding a bird and a skull respectively are often named as Vasistha (Lutoufanzhi) 鹿头梵志 and Mrgasirsa (Bosouxian) 婆薮仙, although this identification has been questioned.

24: TG304-15:49

Arm fragment

Limestone, length 14 cm

This is the fragment of the lower right arm of a Buddhist fig.ure. It has rounded cutting surfaces. The arm was raised horizontally, holding up the fold of a robe. It should date to the Northern Qi period（fig. 65.3, pl. 58.1）.

25: TG304-15:4

Base fragment

Limestone, height 23 cm

This is a fragment of the rounded base of a standing image. It has rounded cutting surfaces. Part of the right foot and the tenon are broken off. The remaining left foot appears fleshy and voluminous. The fragment should date to the Northern Qi period（fig. 66.1, pl. 58.4）.

26: TG304-15:45

Base fragment

Limestone, height 16 cm

This is the fragment of a base of a standing image. Two slender feet are still preserved. The toes of the right foot and part of the tenon are missing. The base fragment should date to the Northern Qi period （fig. 65.3, pl. 58.1）.

27: TG304-15:65

Base fragment

Limestone, height 13 cm

This is the fragment of a fig.ure base. Only the front of the pedestal, two feet of a standing fig.ure, and the tenon are preserved. The surface of the base is finely polished while the surface of the tenon is roughly carved. The object was part of a fig.ure dating to the Northern Qi period （fig. 66.4, pl. 58.6）.

28: TG105-15:5

Lower torso of a Buddha

Limestone, height 20 cm

The fragment shows the pelvic area and part of the left leg of a Buddha. The thin garments do not display any folds and closely follow the outline of the slender body. The image dates to the Northern Qi period（fig. 67.6, pl. 59.4）.

29: TG304-15:77

Torso of a Buddha

Limestone, height 12 cm

Of this torso, the back and a part of the front surface are still extant. The free-standing Buddha is dressed in a plain robe which is softly following the contours of the slender body. The image dates to the Northern Qi period（fig. 67.7, pls. 59.5–6）.

30: TG304-15:33

Torso of a Buddha

Limestone, height 20 cm

Shoulders, chest and back of the Buddha are well preserved. The body is slender and well-modelled. The left shoulder was covered by a coat the hems of which are still extant on the front and back. The image dates to the Northern Qi period（fig. 68.3, pl. 60.4）.

31: T434-69:1

Fig.ure base with inscription

Limestone, 24.5 cm square, height 8.5 cm

The fig.ure base is polished on all four sides. The top shows a square recession about 16 cm wide and half a centimetre deep. The underside is roughly cut.

The front and left face shows an inscription of 63 characters placed in a rectangular grid of finely incised lines. The inscription reads:

大齊天統」四年三月」丙申朔八」日癸卯清」信士佛弟」子張机張」昌兄弟二」人知富可」崇恐身无」常葛(割)舍家」珍上為忘(亡)」父母敬造」

On the left side it continues: 觀世」音像」一軀願」生生世世」常與佛會.

"In the fourth year of the Tiantong era of Great Qi (568), during the New Moon in the third month with the cyclical characters *bingshen shuo*, on the eighth day with the cyclical characters *guimao*, the purely believing followers of the Buddha, the two brothers Zhang Ji and Zhang Chang, knowing that riches can be amassed in great numbers and fearing that the bodily presence has no permanence, split and donated the heirlooms of their family, and for the sake of their deceased parents reverently made an image of Guanyin. May they for ever and ever be united with the Buddha."（figs. 69.5–6, pls. 60.5–7）.

32: TG304-56、57:1

Fragment of a standing bodhisattva

Limestone, height 15.5 cm

The fragment shows the lower torso of a standing bodhisattva. The robe softly follows the outline of the legs. Above the knees, some rhythmic folds of the stole are visible. The undecorated reverse side is slightly rounded, indicating that the fig.ure was free-standing. The object dates to the Northern Qi period （figs. 69.1–2, pl. 60.8）.

33: TG305-58:2

Fragment of a Buddha head

Limestone, height 7 cm

The fragment shows the left side of a Buddha head. The skin surface is smoothly polished. The finely curved eyelids are half closed. The Buddha appears to gaze downwards as if in meditation. The hair is curled into small dots. The object dates to the Northern Qi period （fig. 70.1, pl. 60.9）.

34: TG304-15:84

Hand fragment

Limestone, height 8 cm

The fragment shows two hands laid together. Of the right hand four fingers and of the left one four fingers and the thumb with its fingernail are preserved. The tips of most fingers are missing. Both the original surfaces and the broken sections are weathered. The date of the fragment cannot be discerned. It may have been part of a fig.ure shown in veneration （fig. 62.1, pl. 55.4）.

35: TG304-15:90

Hand fragment

Limestone, height 6 cm

This is the right hand of a fig.ure. The surface is finely polished and the palm shows finely engraved lines. The object dates to the 6th century （fig. 67.1, pl. 59.1）

36: TG304-15:71

Lower torso of a Buddha

Limestone, height 27 cm

This fragment shows the reverse side of a free-standing Buddha. The hem of the coat and a part of the lower garment are visible. The image dates to the Northern Qi period.

Since style, size, the material and the characteristics of the breaks match the ones of the upper torso described before (no 29, 15.77) both objects may have been parts of the same image.

37: TG304-15:98

Fragment of a dragon head

Limestone, height 5 cm

The relief shows the eye, fur, ear and part of the snout of a dragon. The tip of the jaw and the neck are broken off. Besides of these two fragmented areas, all sides of the object are smoothly polished and have been worked in the round. Apparently this object was a part of an openwork relief（figs. 68.4–5）.

38: TG305-58:1

Head of a *feitian*

Limestone, height 4.5 cm

The head is facing to the right. Its face is finely carved shows a smiling mouth and high-ridged nose. Long hair is parted on the forehead and runs down behind the ears. Behind the head a volute is visible which may have belonged to a larger ornament. The head may have been part of the relief decoration of a mandorla. The object dates to the 6th century（fig. 70.2, pls. 61.1–2）.

39: T414-12:2

Fragment of a halo

Limestone, height 12 cm

The polished front face of the halo was originally covered with painting and gilding. Some faint traces of the grounding of a 0.5 cm wide band encircling the head of the fig.ure are still visible. The reverse face of the halo is slightly rounded. In the center a deep, wedge-shaped incision indicates that the halo had once been repaired. The object dates to the 6th century（fig. 70.3, pls. 61.4–5）.

40: T414-12:1

Lotos stand

Limestone, height 9.5 cm, width 14.5 cm

The stand consists of an open lotos flower with a double row of petals on a square base. The round hole in the centre has a diameter of 4.2 cm. The hole was used to insert the tenon of a fig.ure or stele. The surface is severely eroded（fig. 70.4, pls. 61.8–9）.

41: T434-181:5

Fragment of an inscription

Limestone, width 6 cm

The smoothly polished surface shows a grid of fine lines. In the squares of the grid, the character *fa* 法 – the Buddhist law – and remains of two more characters are visible. As the grid is not continued to the left, this appears to have been part of the last line on the left side of an inscription（fig. 70.5）.

42: T413-BK:1

Fragment of a mandorla

Limestone, height 33 cm

The object was found when clearing the terrace border south of the central platform. The high relief decoration on the front face shows the border of a mandorla consisting of five flat parallel bands, and a part of the circular head halo of a fig.ure. The halo consists of one 4 cm wide band with floral decoration and two narrower, undecorated concentric bands. The reverse face bears fine line incisions of indistinct content. The fragment dates to the 6th century（fig. 72, pls. 61.6–7）.

b）Stone fig.ure fragments collected before the excavation

In the years preceding the excavation local farmers found a number of images – reportedly several dozen – when repairing the current road at the bottom of the valley next to the river. 26 of these fragments were secured by staff of Linqu museum and by members of the excavation team. In the catalogue we mark these objects with a "C".

43: C:123

Fragment of the sculpture donated by monk Bao 宝

Limestone, height 25 cm

The object is a fragment of the upper left section of a mandorla. Only one face of this nearly triangular object is undamaged and shows a part of the border of the mandorla. The front bears floral decoration and a flame ornament in low relief. Below and to the right small sections of the halos a bodhisattva and a Buddha are still discernible. At the top of the object the two knees of a *feitian* in high relief are visible. The reverse side shows a finely carved inscription of which seven lines with 17 characters are still extant. The inscription reads "比丘宝□（爽）……」大魏孝昌……」五日壬……」法社□（政）……」三老……」孙……」□……" The fragmentary text contains part of the name of a monk named Bao, apparently the donor, and the reign period *xiaochang* of the Northern Wei which lasted from 525 to 527 AD（figs. 73.3–5, pls. 63.4–5）.

44: C:125

Limestone, height 44 cm, thickness 14 cm

This is part of the tip of a mandorla. The right border of the fragment is still relatively complete. The high relief shows a segment of a halo and a flying *feitian*. Below the flying scarfs of a second *feitian* are still discernible. Above one can see the snake-like body of a dragon with upward-facing tail. The dragon spits out the stem of a lotos flower. The blossom of the lotos connects with the lotos decoration in the outer band of the halo below, forming a consecutive floral ornament. The design is arranged to give the impression that the dragon is spitting out an endless flow of lotos flowers. This playful treatment of the dragon-and-lotos motif can also be found in the decoration of a stele from Longxing temple in Qingzhou that is dated by inscription to 533 AD (Stele of the nun Hui Zhao 惠照, see Wang Huaqing ed., *Buddhist*

Sculptures – New Discoveries from Qingzhou, Shandong Province, Hong Kong Museum of Art 2001, pp. 154–155.) Four late Northern Wei fig.ure steles with the motif were collected in Guangrao, one of which is dated to 527 (see *Wenwu* 1996/12, pp. 75–82, fig.s. 1–4 and 6–9). The reverse side of the mandorla is undecorated. The fragment should date to the late Northern Wei （figs. 74.2–3, pl. 63.6）.

45: C:117

Fragment of a mandorla

Limestone, height 6.5 cm

The front face of the mandorla reveals a segment of a halo engraved with three concentric bands as well as a small segment of a body mandorla that was bordered by three more bands. To the right the damaged surface indicates the area where the head of a fig.ure had been connected to the mandorla. The reverse shows a part of an inscription. Two lines with seven characters are still legible: "……兴和二年……」……丁丑朔……" The text includes the date "second year of the *xinghe* era" of the Eastern Wei, referring to the year 540 （figs. 74.1, 76.5, pls. 64.5–6）.

46: C:114

Standing bodhisattva

Limestone, height 42 cm

The bodhisattva formed part of a three-fig.ure stele and was positioned to the left of the Buddha image. The bodhisattva wears a high crown with long ribbons running down on both sides. His right hand is raised in *abhaya* mudra, the other lowered in *varada* mudra. The girdle around the robe is closed with an ornamental knot to which a pendant is attached. On the chest, some traces of a necklace and inner garments are visible. The ends of a long stole fall down on both sides. Parts of the mandora are preserved on which faint remains of the snake-like body of a dragon can be discerned. The reverse side is undecorated. The object should date to the Eastern Wei or Northern Qi periods （fig. 74.5, pl. 64.4）.

47: C:110

Fragment of a fig.ure stele

Limestone, height 34 cm

The front face of the fragment shows remains of a standing Buddha and the feet of a bodhisattva to his left. The feet of the Buddha are resting on a round base. The bodhisattva stands on a base in the shape of a lotos bud above two lotos petals. Between both fig.ures a dragon in wild movement is visible. The dragon stretches his front legs with the paws touching the fig.ure bases. Head and neck are thrown back, facing the Bodhisattva. The upper body, front legs, and neck of the dragon are carved in openwork technique. The fragment should date to the Northern Qi period （fig. 76.4, pl. 65.3）.

48: C:120

Lower torso of a standing bodhisattva

Limestone, height 23

The fragment of bodhisattva is carved in the round as a free-standing image. It is dressed in a long skirt that is fixed above the waist by a girdle. The stole is laid crosswise over the body and held together by a round ornamental disk. A long pearl chain further decorates the torso. The image dates to the Northern Qi period（figs. 76.1–3, pls. 66.1–2）.

49: C:118

Lower torso of a Buddha

Limestone, height 19.5 cm

The fragment is worked in the round, indicating that the Buddha was free-standing. The sleeve falling down on one side of the fragment suggests that the fig.ure was raising its left hand. The robe shows no folds and closely follows the slender outline of the body. The image dates to the Northern Qi period （fig. 79.2, pl. 67.5）.

50: C:1

Fragment of a mandorla

Limestone, height 5.5 cm

The small fragment of a mandorla shows part of an instrument, apparently a lute. One hand and part of the flying stole of the *feitian* that played the instrument are still visible. The reverse side is polished but undecorated. The object dates to the 6th century （fig. 73.1, pls. 63.1–2）.

51: C:3

Base fragment with fig.ure foot

Lime stone, width 10 cm

The fragment of a round base still retains the front part of the right foot of a fig.ure. The rounded foot is finely shaped with all toes of nearly equal width. The upper surface of the base and the foot are finely polished and barely weathered while the damaged reverse side is strongly eroded. After the image was destroyed the fragment was likely lying upside down on the ground and was exposed to the environment for a long time before the fragment was finally placed in a pit. The top part was well protected while its reverse side became eroded （fig. 73.2 ）.

52: C:101

Lotos base

Limestone, height 20.5 cm, diameter 42 cm

The large stand is decorated with three layers of downward-facing lotos petals. The top shows an eight-sided recession. The body of this base has been carefully chiselled out, leaving a wall thickness of only 4–6 cm（pl. 63.3）.

53: C:115

Head of a Buddha fig.ure

Limestone, height 37.2 cm

The Buddha head has a high *usnisa*. The hair forms curls and runs down in long streaks to both sides of the head. The eye brows are carved in fine curves; the eyes are slightly closed but directed at the viewer. The mouth below the high-ridged nose forms a slight smile. The cheeks are full and rounded. The smooth reverse of the head is worked in the round, indicating that the head belonged to a free-standing statue. The head dates to the Eastern Wei to Northern Qi period, or the middle of the 6th century.（fig. 74.4, pls. 64.1–3）.

54: C:122

Fragment of a mandorla

Limestone, height 40.4 cm

The front face of the fragment shows a section of the body mandorla of a Buddha to the left, a part of the body of a dragon, and the hems of the robes of a Bodhisattva to the right. The body mandorla has a border of five concentric bands, encircled by a wider band with faint floral decoration. The reverse side is decorated in low relief. In the centre stands a person dressed in a long monk's robe, shown frontally. The person holds a high cylindrical box in his hand. To the left, a part of a second person in a monk's robe is visible, presenting a large round dish or plate. The second person is turned towards its left, facing the first. To the right the corner of an angular stool or throne, part of a lotos pedestal and some remains of a fig.ure are visible. The scene apparently showed a holy image that was attended by several monks carrying gifts. The object dates to the 6th century (figs. 75.1–3, pls. 65.1–2).

55: C:109

Fragment of a fig.ure stele

Limestone, height 40.0 cm

The fragment shows a dragon in high relief. The dragon streches out a paw with three claws. The head is shown from the side, with eye, mouth, ear and fur clearly visible. The dragon spits out a bunch of lotos stems which open into blossoms. The lotos probably supported the stand of a Bodhisattva. The fragment was apparently part of the lower left side of a three-fig.ure stele. The image dates to the late Northern or the Eastern Wei period (figs. 77.1–2, pls. 66.4–5).

56: C:121

Fragment of a mandorla

Limestone, height 10 cm

The front face of the mandorla is polished and incised with fine lines. The decoration shows part of a body mandorla. Its border consists of one wide band with floral decoration and five smaller undecorated bands. To the right follows a row of lotos petals. To the upper right a small section of a halo with floral decoration is visible. The fragmented area of the surface to the right indicates the spot where the head of the Buddha had been broken off. To the left a small section of a lotos halo in high relief remains that probably belonged to a bodhisattva. The image can be dated to the 6th century（figs. 77.3–4, pl. 65.4）.

57: C:124

Fragment of a mandorla

Limestone, height 20 cm

The polished surface of the mandorla is engraved with fine lines. To the left it shows a segment of a halo, ornamented with several concentric bands and a lotos flower in high relief. Below the halo are remains of body mandorla that is encircled by a wide band with floral decoration, five narrower undecorated bands, and a row of lotos petals. To the right, a section of a circle that might be the border of another halo is visible. The decoration of the body mandorla closely resembles the one of no. 56/C:121. As the bands are of different sizes the fragments cannot have belonged to the same fig.ure but it is likely that both were made in the same workshop at about the same time. The image dates to the 6th century（figs. 77.5–6, pl. 65.5）.

58: C:107

Lotos base with inscription

Limestone, height 14.5 cm, diameter 30 cm

The round base is covered by an opened lotos flower with double-layered voluminous petals. The lower part of the base bears an inscription of 52 characters in 13 rows："故人王□苻」妻石男□」故人王宝林」故人惠明」妻焦男□」林妻李绯(？)」…". The inscription gives a long list of names: Two men surnamed Wang and a certain Hui with four of their wives and six of their children. These are probably the names of donors（figs. 78.1–2, pl. 67.6）.

59: C:116

Base of an image commissioned by Sun Wen

Limestone, height 23 cm

A lotos flower with two rows of voluminous petals covers the square base with a round central hole. One face of the base bears an inscription with 32 characters in six rows. Nine characters are illegible.

"□平七年四月」八日孙文敬造」□潘为亡息阿」□造像一躯□」□□生天□□」□福」" The inscription records the date "day eight of the fourth month of the seventh year of X-*ping* era" which should refer to the period *wuping* 武平 of Northern Qi and the year 576. The name of the donor is certain Sun Wen 孙文 who commissioned the image for the sake of his deceased child (figs. 78.3–4, pls. 67.1–2).

60: C:108

Lotos base

Limestone, height 21 cm

A lotos flower with two rows of voluminous unpartitioned petals opens above a circular base. The stand dates to the 6th century (fig. 78.5, pl. 67.3).

61: C:111

Fragment of a halo

Limestone, diameter 14.5 cm

The object is the central part of a circular halo. The damaged surface in the centre indicates the spot where the head and neck of a fig.ure connected to the halo. The reverse side is smooth and slightly rounded. The border of this object bears rather particular features. Several areas to the left, top left and top right are smoothly finished while the sections in-between are damaged and broken off. This indicates that the halo was much larger originally, and that the area beyond the central part still extant was carved in openwork technique. No further examples of such a skilful treatment of a halo are known from sites in Shandong province. The object should date to the 6th century (fig. 79.1, pl. 67.4).

c) Ceramic fig.ure fragments

62: T413-70:5

Standing bodhisattva

White buff ceramic, height 7.5 cm

Base tenon and head of the fig.ure are broken off. The bodhisattva is standing upright with the right hand raised and the left arm stretched. The right hand holds a rounded object between thumb and index finger which may be a lotos bud. The object placed in the left hand is lost. It may have been a flask as some buff ceramic fig.ures from other Shandong sites include this item. The bodhisattva wears a long skirt and a loin cloth with a girdle tied in a knot. The robes follow the outline of his body. A pearl necklace adorns the neck. Pearl strings run crosswise over the torso. A stole covers both shoulders and runs down to the sides of the body. The reverse side shows several finger imprints. Apparently the object was pressed in a mould before firing. The object should date to the Northern Qi period (figs. 80.1–2, pl. 62.1).

63: T414-74:2

Fragment of a Bodhisattva

White buff ceramic, height 5.5 cm

Base tenon and torso of the Bodhisattva are broken off. The fig.ure is standing upright with the feet slightly parted. It is dressed with a skirt and a stole. The thin cloth of the skirt reveals the outline of the legs below. The reverse side shows finger imprints indicating that the object was pressed into a mould. The bodhisattva should date to the Northern Qi period（fig. 80.3, pl. 62.2）.

64: T413-181:4

Fig.ure stand

White buff ceramic, width 4 cm

The mall stand is broken into four parts. On a two-level square base an open lotos covers the central hole where the tenon of a fig.ure was to be inserted. The lotos has double-lobed petals. The stand was apparently pressed in a mould before firing（fig. 80.5, pl. 62.5）.

65: TG304-C:1

Fig.ure stand

White buff ceramic

The small fragment of a base shows an open lotos flower with voluminous petals over a two-tier square base. The stand was pressed in a mould. (figs. 69.1–2, pl. 62.4)

66: TG413-178:2

Fragment of ceramic lotos-shaped stand

Grey earthenware, height 19.5 cm

The fragmented circular stand has a round opening in the centre. The original outer diameter was about 78 cm and the wall thickness 12 cm. The stand is made resembling a lotos blossom with four layers of upward-facing petals above a circular base. Each petal is about 10 cm wide.

The base is made of coarse grey earthenware. The material resembles the ware used for tiles and bricks of the temple. It is possible that this stand was made and fired locally, perhaps at one of the kilns found to the north east of the temple site. The base was hand-shaped without the help of a mould（fig. 80.4, pl. 61.3）.

67: T434-201:6

Seated Buddha

Grey earthenware, height 7.5

The image is sitting cross-legged on a round stool or base. The right hand is raised in *abhaya* mudra, the other is lowered in *varada* mudra. The extremities are rather voluminous. The robe covers only the left shoulder and the left arm. Its hem is running across the chest. On the chest, the hem of an inner garment is visible. The fig.ure sits in front of a mandorla the top of which is broken off. The mandorla was decorated with a band of floral ornaments. The reverse side is roughly finished and slightly rounded. Apparently the fig.ure was shaped by hand, not in a mould. Since the material used resembles the coarse grey material of the bricks and tiles of the temple, it is possible that this fig.ure was made at the site, possibly in one of the brick kilns northeast of the temple. As the object is modelled very roughly it is hard to date. It may have been made during the Tang dynasty（fig. 80.6, pl. 62.3）.

5. Chronology and date

Ceramics

Most of the high-fired ceramics excavated at the White Dragon site were celadon, white, and black wares. Only a few *sancai* (three-coloured), dark brown, yellow and green wares came to light.

The large number of celadons came in two different qualities. Some had impurities in the bodies and the green glaze contained black spots. Their outer walls were incompletely glazed and often showed drip lines (pls. 39.6, 46.3–4). The higher quality celadon wares were made from purer clay that had a greenish-grey tone. The glaze was thin and glossy (pls. 47.1–2).

The glaze of most of the white wares had a greenish tone and showed crazing; the body contained inclusions in straw colour. The fragments had pure white bodies that were coated with slips and fired at high temperature (pls. 39.1–2).

The glaze of the black wares was thin and had a reddish brown tone (pl. 49). Only two pieces of *sancai* wares were found (pl. 51). Yellow and green wares again came in small numbers. Their bodies were softer and more porous and their glazes were crazed. They invariably belonged to *hu* 壶 bottles.

The vessel shapes included bowls, jars, *bo* (钵 monks' bowls) and bottles. Some bowls had a larger or smaller cookie-shaped foot, that is a flat round foot without recession in the centre (pl. 39.5). In some cases the area inside the foot was slightly recessed. A small number of the vessels showed a *bi*-disc foot, that is a wide ring foot with a distinct recession in the centre (pls. 43.2, 4, 6). Two ring-shaped feet fragments of white porcelain wares were found. Their bodies were pure and white and had been fired at high temperature(pl. 44. 1). The dark brown wares had a ring foot that was always unglazed in the centre.

The earthenware can be sorted into two groups. Group A included wares with brown, in greenish-gray, or red body. The vessel types mainly included basins with wide flat rims, bowls, monk's bowls *bo* , steaming pots, jars with lugs and inclined rims, urns with folded rims, and urns with evert rims (figs. 39, 40, 41). Group B had a grey body and included basins with narrowly folded or evert rims, and jars with curved rims (fig. 42).

The cultural layers 64, 70, 195, 69 and 68 contained large numbers of shards. The finds shall be briefly characterized.

Most of the shards found in layer 64 were celadon wares that belonged to two categories. Category A had a body that contained many inclusions. The material was thick and heavy. The fluid glaze was a deep bean-green that showed black spots. Most shards were fragments of bowls and bottles with a flat round cookie foot and three spur marks on the inside. These wares can be dated to the Northern Qi dynasty (pl. 50). Category B had a greenish-grey body. Some of the jars had bodies with reddish brown outer surface, and their thin and glossy glaze was greenish grey. Most vessels had a round cookie foot which was slightly recessed. The material was generally lighter and thinner than in category A. These wares can be dated to the Tang dynasty (pls. 46.5, 47). Many shards of black wares as well as fragments of a high-stemmed plate dou of sancai ware were founded in layer 64. The fragments of a high-stemmed plate dou of sancai ware can be dated to the late Tang dynasty. In conclusion, layer 64 contained shards of various dates. The layer grew over a long period of time during which the site was actively used.

Layer 70 included hardly any celadon wares of category A but brought to light large numbers of category B. In addition, one celadon shard with condensed and heavy body and a glossy crazed glaze was found that was different from the categories mentioned above. A great amount of black wares were excavated. The layer also included one shard of a white ware bowl (pls. 39.4-5). One fragment had a bi-disc shaped foot. This should be a layer of late Tang date.

Layer 69 mainly contained white wares.

Most of the shards in layer 68 and 69 were white wares. They often had three spur marks. The glaze was of yellowish or greenish-grey tones and showed some crazing. Very few celadon wares were found. The two layers can be connected as they contained fitting fragments of white ware bowls. The earthenware objects mainly had grey bodies. The typology includes basins with narrow and folded rims as well as jars with curved rims and angular, bridge-shaped lugs.

Layers 19, 21 and 5 contained fewer shards. Finds included white wares, dark-brown wares, and wares with green and yellow painted decoration. The jars and bowls had a ring foot that was unglazed in the centre.

The ceramic finds date to four different periods. The first period includes celadon wares of category A as well as the reddish brown earthenware bowls and bowls with flat cookie-shaped feet found in layer 64. These finds date to Northern Qi. The second period comprises celadon wares of category B of layers 64, 70, and 195. These should date to the Tang dynasty. The third period includes the ceramics found in layers 69 and layer 68. These should date to the Song dynasty. The fourth period includes the ceramics from layers 21, 19, and 5. They date to the Jin and Yuan dynasties or later.

Where were the ceramics manufactured? Most of the shards, including the celadon, the white, black, and dark brown wares as well as wares decorated in green and yellow are from kilns in Zibo 淄博 in central Shandong. The celadon bottle with dense and heavy body and glossy crazed glaze that was found in layer 70 (70:20) quite possibly came from kilns in Henan. Those celadon wares with greenish-grey dense body and thin celadon glaze (for instance 70:106) were not local wares but came quite possibly from kilns in south of China. This indicates that the people who used the site interacted with various and sometimes distant regions.

Stratigraphy

The landscape of the area under investigation has been remodelled several times in its history. The temple reshaped a usage horizon of the 5th to 3rd centuries BC, and later periods of use removed all above-ground traces of the temple architecture. To understand the history of the site one needs to investigate the layers of deposits to the north and south of the central platform.

a) Northern area of the central platform

The first phase: At the outset of phase one, a platform with a surrounding trench was dug out of the living loess. The south face of the platform and the trench borders were then lined with fired bricks. A small building to the west and two kilns to the east were erected. Later layers will help to understand the original situation better (fig. 11).

The temple was used for a long time during which the ground surface of the trench was kept free from rubble or sediments. Only the relatively thin layer 223 came in. In a second stage, layer 64 covered the ground of the trench. The layer consisted of large amounts of tiles. Judging from the eve plates, all but one of which were of type A, the layer should be the result of the slow collapse of a single building with a roof that had eve plates of type A. Several fragments of ceramics were found that date mainly to the 6th and early 7th century. One fragment of *sancai* ware was found that should date to the eighth century (pl. 51). The layer contained no fig.ure fragments.

On top of 64, layer 70 came in. Near the north wall of the trench layer 70 was up to 50 cm high, in the south it reached up to 12 cm. The layer apparently came in from the north. It contained large amounts of tiles. Since most of the eve plates were of type B, the layer should come from a different roof or building than layer 64. The layer came in quickly, with little earth or sand sediment between the tiles. Some tiles were piled up in stacks, suggesting that the layer was the result of a sudden collapse of a roof that fell directly into the trench. A part of the northern trench wall caved in as well. Three fragments of Buddhist statues were found in the rubble. Between the tiles fragments of ceramics of the Northern dynasties and the Tang period (6th – 9th centuries) were found. The youngest fragment was a part of a bowl with white body (70:3, pl. 39.4) dating to the late Tang period. The layer should belong to the 9th or 10th centuries.

On top came layer 195. It contained bricks, tiles and plaster fragments. It grew in thickness towards the south. It was formed from the rubble of a building on the central platform. There is no sign of a walking horizon. It mainly included Tang period ceramic fragments and should date to the late Tang period or slightly later, that is the 9th or 10th century.

The second phase: The next layer indicating use is layer 69. The layer was levelled and had a used surface. A large fireplace (164) belonged to the layer. 69 was a living surface used for a long time. One large plaster fragment was found that appears to have fallen off a wall in one piece (157/158, pl. 32.1). The layer further contained the square base of a Buddhist image dated by inscription to the year 4 of the Tiantong reign of Northern Qi, that is 568 (69:1, figs. 69.5–6). The layer contained mainly Tang period ceramic shards. The latest ceramic find was a fragment of a bowl with white body, dating to the early Northern Song period (69:101, pl. 42.3). The layer should belong to the early Northern Song, the 10th to 11th century.

Layers 117 and 118 ran over layer 69. These layers mainly contained sand, some burned earth and plaster fragments. These layers may be sediments that were swept into the trench from the hill slope.

Layer 68 was a thick layer consisting of fine sand. It was level and contained a fire pit (122), indicating long-term use. The small stone wall (22) running diagonally through the former trench was built in this layer. The layer contained some fragments of Buddhist images and some rubble from buildings. The ceramic finds consisted of Tang and Song ceramics. The latest find were fragments of two white ware bowls which date to late Northern Song (early 12th century, 68.16 and 68.2. pls. 40.3–4). Layer 68 was a horizon of use that came in over a relatively long period of time.

The third phase: Layer 5 covered a large area. It ran over most of the trench (that was filled in by then) as well as over part of the central terrace. It further covered the remaining parts of the brick walls. The layer grew over a long time period. It contained large amounts of brick and tile fragments as well as ceramic shards. The shards mainly belonged to the Tang and Song period. The layer belongs to the Jin or Yuan period, that is the late 12th to 13th century or later.

Above layer 5 layer 4 set in. The layer also covered a large area. It was rather strong and came in over a long period of time. It contained brick and tile fragments as well as ceramics. Some shards of blue-and-white *qinghua* porcelains indicate that the layer grew over the Ming period and the following decades (14th to 17th centuries). Above layer 4 the modern plough layer set in.

b) Southern area of the central platform

The first phase: The surface of the ground to the south of the walls of the central platform and the pathways was levelled. There were no signs of a walking surface. First a small brick wall was added at meter 1045.6, running north-south. At the time of excavation it was still 0.8 m long and four layers high. Part of the wall had collapsed (pl. 26.2). The function of this brick wall is unclear. It is possible that it was part of an early entrance situation. It was built when the temple was in use.

Slightly later layer 188 came in. In front of the centre of the central platform it was strongest and measured up to 50 cm. To the west its thickness declined. The eastern side was destroyed by a later footpath. The layer consisted of compressed, grey earth. It contained a few brick and tile fragments but no ceramic shards or image fragments. It came in when the temple was in use and may have been part of an entrance situation.

The remains of two walls set in on top of layer 188 (165 and 166, pl. 27). They ran in a north-south direction and consisted of stones and bricks. The eastern one at m 1058 leaned to the west and was still preserved to a length of 0.88 m and a height of 0.4 m. The western one at m 1054.6 leaned to the east and was still 0.9 m long and 0.3 m high. Both walls were 3.52 m apart. They were built at the same time and belong together. Because they are positioned precisely in the middle of the brick wall of the central terrace it is imaginable that the walls were part of a new entrance situation. The entrance or ramp would have been formed of both walls and layers 187 and 186. Both layers contained very few brick and tile fragments. The layers date to the time the temple was in use (fig. 27).

The second phase: This access or ramp was later extended to the west. At m 1050.8 a wall made of large stone slabs (74) was added that was 2.9 m long and up to 1.06 m high. The area between this wall and the former entrance situation was then filled with layers 175 and 176 that contained large amounts of brick and tile fragments and some ceramics. The wall and both layers should date to a time after the destruction of a temple building. As the area east of wall 165 has been damaged by the recent foot path it is unclear if the entrance was extended to that side as well.

Later the stone wall 73 was added at m 1053.7. The wall was built in a pit inside the layers 175 and 176 and should be later than wall 74. To the west of wall 74 layer 181 was deposited. Layer 181 showed signs of use of the site. It included cattle teeth, several bones and a mussel shell.

The third phase: After wall 73 was destroyed, more layers with large amounts of rubble, tile and brick fragments came in to both side of the stone wall (layers 178–180 and 174). Layer 178 contained ceramic shards of the Song period. Since the layers above this group of layers only contained small amounts of bricks and tiles, it should belong to the time when the platform was finally cleared of the building remains. Layer 167 appears to have been added to level the ground, perhaps as bottoming for agricultural use.

After layer 178 and 174 were brought in (both can be connected by the discovery fitting shards of the same ceramic object), the surface of the trench was level with the surface of the central platform and the top brick layer of the remaining southern wall. At this point, bricks were removed from the southern wall layer by layer, leaving a pit (pit 15, fig. 10.1) in the width of the wall and up to 80 cm deep (that is as deep as a man's arm can reach from the surface). The high-quality bricks of the south wall were probably re-used for peasant houses in the village. Pit 15 was then filled with rubble from the buildings, a large amount fig.ure fragments, and dark earth containing ash and other signs of use.

Pit 15 was then covered by layer 54 which consisted of sand and contained very few ceramic shards and stone fragments. Above layer 54 the current plough layer set in.

Conclusion

History of the site

Over the last two millennia the site had been used several times. It was possible to define three stages of activity: During stage one the trench was kept clean and the buildings were in a good state of repair. Later during this stage layer 64 and 70 came in which are the results of the slow collapse of the building on the central platform and a building to the north of the trench. Next to tiles, layer 64 contained no and layer 70 contained only a single fragment of a brick. Finds of ceramics confirmed that these layers grew over the 6th to 10th centuries. A second stage of use began with layer 69. This stage left several pits and fireplaces and may have been considerably later than the first one. The third stage of use began with layer 68. As the layer contained ceramic shards of the Northern Song period (960–1127) it had likely come in during or after the 12th century. Modern plough layers covered this horizon. The tomb described above that cut through layers of all three stages indicates the possibility of additional periods of use.

The various phases in the stratigraphy of the areas to the north and to the south of the central platform are difficult to correlate as no layer continuously runs over the complete site. All were interrupted by the platform and the eastern and western pathways. However, it is still possible to identify comparable situations in both locations.

When the walls 65 and 66 were built, the building on the central platform was still standing. The extension of the entrance situation to the west includes large amounts of tiles and was built when the temple buildings started to decay. Layer 181 adjoining wall 74 on the western side contained bones and signs of long-term activity at the site. This should mean that the extension of the entrance situation and the deposition of 181 may correspond to the long-term usage horizon of layers 69 and 68 in the north. The later clearing of the remaining ruins of the platform and the deposition of Buddhist images in pit 15 should therefore coincide with the beginnings of phase 3 of the northern situation, which is layer 5 that dated to the 12th and 13th centuries.

6. Discussion and conclusions

Buildings remains

During the 6th century the site consisted of several areas. One platform of a building was found. The platform was surrounded by a trench to protect it against the water that floods down from the hill slopes to the north during rainstorms. The water would then escape through the two water outlets to the south. This protection was necessary. When working on the site, our team experienced two severe thunderstorms during which the excavation trenches filled to the rim with water and mud.

The borders of the platform and of the trench were lined with bricks. The bricks used at the site mainly had one standardised size. They were probably made in the kilns next to the temple. The bricks were of varying quality. Apparently the best bricks with straight faces were selected to build the south wall of the central terrace. The bricks of this wall were all of a light grey colour and had been polished after firing. They were stacked up with barely any gap between courses. The remaining walls, on the other hand, included bricks that were of uneven surface, discoloured, or incomplete. The south wall of the central platform was built to a superior standard probably because it was visible when one approached the temple from the village. This wall was made to be seen.

Most of the walls were a single brick strong. Only the south wall was double skinned. All walls were built dry, without the use of mortar. The brick walls had no structural function and were not made to support any roof. They served merely as protection and embellishment of the trench and the terrace borders.

No ruins of the buildings on the platforms survived. All information needs to be gathered from the layout of the site, the remaining brick walls, and from the rubble that accumulated in the trench and in front of the southern wall.

Some valuable information can be assembled when inspecting the tiles found in the trench. From the small number of bricks and the large number of tiles found inside the trench we learn that the building or buildings had tiled roofs while the walls were built of mud or wood, but not of bricks. The tiles were made in two standardised sizes, narrow ones and wide ones. The narrow and wide varieties were without doubt used as "monk and nun" tiles. The roof would be consisting of alternating rows of large and narrow tiles, with the "monk" tiles forming prominent ridges on the surface. The wide tiles would overlap. The tenons of the narrow tiles would fit into the following tile, forming smooth rows without visible overlappings. On the eves the "monk" tiles had ornamental end plates as is still the case in more recent architecture.

No tiles cut in angled or other special shapes were found that would suggest the use of hipped roofs. The roof or roofs were probably gabled.

Nearly all eve plates were of type A or type B. The buildings of the site were mainly decorated with these two types of *wadang*. When counting *wadang* that were complete or preserved to more than 50%, 42 were of type A and 76 of type B. It is possible that the two types of *wadang* belonged to two different buildings. If we assume that one building was solely equipped with a single type of *wadang*, we can get a rough idea of the size of the roof parts the *wadang* of which have been recovered. The distance between two *wadang* would have been about 42 cm. Taken together, the *wadang* of type A would indicate a minimum eve length of the building of 17.60 m, while the *wadang* of type B would give a running length of the eve of nearly 32 m.

The existence of eve plates of types C, D, E and F of which only one to two specimens each were found is rather puzzling. Types E and F were made by a technology uncommon at this temple. Types D, E and F had sizes that would not fit the roofs made with the standard tiles of the site. They belonged to other buildings. Furthermore, their number is too small to suggest that buildings existed on the site that had roofs which were made exclusively with tiles of their sizes. It appears as if these tiles were brought to the site from other temples. One may even imagine that these tiles served as samples for craftsmen working in the White Dragon temple. This suggestion is supported by the fact that the eve plates of types A and C closely resembled in size and decoration the eve plates commonly found at Mingdao temple. They also show the same joining technique. The craftsmen building the White Dragon temple probably had made themselves aware of how tiles were made at other temples.

It is further noteworthy that some eve plates showed traces of painting in cold pigment. In addition, many finds of painted plaster fragments indicate that the walls of the buildings were painted. During the 6th and 7th centuries the temple buildings must have looked most colourful.

As customary in traditional Chinese architecture the roof was supported by wooden posts and beams. No remains of this wooden structure were preserved. The lack of any lacquer fragments makes it likely that the beam surfaces were not lacquered. Doors and window frames were embellished with large iron nails. Some fragments of worked stone slabs found on the site indicate that door frames or thresholds had been made of stone.

One smaller building was situated on the adjoining terrace surface to the west. It should date to the time when the temple was in use. The simple structure and its small size as well as the burned ground inside the building suggest that it was a service building rather than a temple hall or a living quarter.

Two observations indicate that more than one large buildings with brick roofs existed at the site. The first is the widespread use of two different types of eve plates. Type A and type B should come from different buildings. Since layer 64 mainly contained type A and layer 70 mainly type B one may even suggest that the buildings collapsed at different times. The second observation regards the special characteristics of layer 70 in the northern section of the trench. The large amount of tiles that came in at the end of phase 1 clearly fell into the trench from the north. In some areas they were piled up in deep stacks with hardly any sand or loess in-between the tiles. Apparently a roof collapsed and fell into the trench in a single event. This suggests that a second building stood right north of the trench that collapsed later than the one on the central platform. Since no signs of a second water trench, a platform or other traces of use were found to the north, one must assume that the surface in this part of the site has been decisively remodelled after the destruction of the building.

After the erection of the southern wall, but when the temple was still active, an entrance was added leading from the south right up to the centre of the terrace. The entrance was mainly made of earth but had a brick lining to both sides.

Two kilns were situated to the north-east, about 27 m away from the terrace border. The find of some bricks inside the kilns and the discovery of a mould fragment of an eve plate suggest that the bricks and tiles for the temple buildings were produced locally. It is worth noting that the find of a half-finished stone sculpture fragment further suggests that the temple included a stone mason's workshop. There were no traces of a surrounding wall or a gate building.

The temple was used over at least 200 years. At some point in the 9th or 10th centuries its sculptures were smashed and scattered, and the buildings dilapidated. The platform was reused several times and the entrance to the south was extended, but no new large buildings with brick roofs were ever erected again. Much later, during the 12th or 13th centuries when the buildings had disappeared completely someone removed bricks from the southern terrace wall, leaving a pit in the ground that was then filled with rubble and the remaining fragments of statues, while other fragments were deposited next to the river in the valley.

Fragments of Buddhist sculptures

At the site of the Temple of the White Dragon more than 200 fragments of stone statues and remains of several ceramic fig.urines were excavated. In the years preceding the excavation, peasants of the local village made chance finds when ploughing their fields and during repairs of the road in the valley directly below the temple site. Of the reportedly several dozen fragments that came to light, 26 were secured by Linqu museum or by members of the excavation team.

a) Stone images

Most stone fig.ures are of the local greyish-white limestone that sometimes shows inclusions in brown and reddish brown. The fine-grained material is easy to cut and polish. It is very similar to the one commonly used in Longxing temple in Qingzhou and other Shandong temples at the time.

Two fragments of Buddhist images (no. 21/70.1 and 15.16) were made of sand stone. Two small fig.ure stele were made of a coarse green chlorite schist with white mica, magnetite and garnet inclusions which is found locally as well. Since both fig.ures resemble in material, size, style and the unrefined ductus of the inscriptions a group of fig.ures recovered from the site of Mingdao temple in the east of Linqu county, one may suggest that these two images were brought here from Mingdao temple (See Linqu Museum ed., 临朐佛教造像艺术 /*Buddhist sculptural art of Linqu*, Beijing, Kexue press 2010, no. 1, 2, 7 and 15). One half-finished fragment was made of talc schist (BK.4, no. 18, fig. 71.1).

The limestone fig.ures were generally hewn from one piece of stone, with a separate stand. In most cases, the fig.ures had a conical tenon by means of which the fig.ure could be inserted into the stand.

The details of the fig.ures were finely carved and the surfaces polished. Some had line engravings added after polishing or traces of open work carving.

Two different cutting procedures can be distinguished. Objects made during the first half of the 6th century display flat cutting surfaces that finish in sharp edges where two surfaces meet. This is especially prominent in the treatment of folds of garments. With the first method, folds were cut in a single run of a flat chisel. Fig.ures made during the second half of the 6th century show smooth rounded cutting surfaces without sharp edges. The lines of the folds in the latter images appear to have been carved with repeated cuts of a chisel that may have had a rounded blade.

Several sculptures bore traces of cold pigments and gilding. Many fig.ures were of very fine craftsmanship.

b) Ceramic images

A few clay fig.ure fragments survived. Two small bodhisattva statues and two fragmented bases were made of white buff ceramic. These objects were produced by pressing the raw material into prefabricated moulds before firing at low temperature. The objects were most probably originally painted in cold pigment. Similar fig.ures were found in the vicinity of Longhua temple in Boxing and occasionally at other sites in Shandong. More are documented in museum collections. 56 were excavated in Boxing alone (see *Shandong baitao fojiao zaoxiang* 山东白陶佛教造像 /Buddhist Statues Made of White Pottery of Shandong Province, Beijing, Wenwu press 2011, p. 9 and passim. See also the unprovenanced find of 1995, published in Linqu Museum ed., *Linqu fojiao zaoxiang yishu* 临朐佛教造像艺术 /Buddhist sculptural art of Linqu, Beijing, Kexue press 2010, no. 87; and the bodhisattva dated to 563, *Inaugural Exhibition Catalog of the Museum of East Asian Art Volume 1: Chinese Ceramics*, Bath, Museum of East Asian Art 1993, fig.s 58–59). Since the fig.ures are made with a clay normally used for porcelain one may assume that white buff ceramic fig.urines were produced at the Zibo 淄博 kilns and then brought to the White Dragon temple and other sites.

One lotos base as well as a possibly later image of a seated Buddha were made of coarse grey material that was also used for bricks and tiles at the site (201.6, no. 67). Both objects were shaped by hand, not in moulds. They may have been made in the brick kilns east of the temple.

c) Size

The sculptures were of various sizes, ranging from a body height of a few centimetres to perhaps 1.5 m. Three fragments may have belonged to fig.ures that were about life size (C.115/ no. 53, 15.4, 54.3). No main image of the temple can be singled out.

d) Number of sculptures

At the time of excavation all fig.ures were broken and damaged. Most were smashed into many small pieces. From the fragments found on the site, only very few could be joined with other fragments or re-assembled into complete fig.ures. Apparently the majority of fragments went missing.

As only a part of the remains of the sculptures originally used at the site are still extant it is difficult to establish an exact number of how many Buddhist fig.ures may have belonged to the temple. One indicator is the amount of conical tenons excavated that joined the fig.ure or stele to its stand, as well as the number of fig.ures recovered with their base still attached. Altogether, 15 fig.ures with stone tenons or separate tenons came to light, next to one object with its base still attached. 13 lime stone stands, one stand of grey brick earthenware, and two small white buffo ceramic stands were found. The minimal number of fig.ures used by the temple was 16. However, since of the more than 200 Fragments only less than ten could be re-joined with other fragments, the original number of sculptures of the White Dragon Temple must have been considerably higher, perhaps up to 100 sculptures.

e) Style

Images from the Bailong site display distinct stages of a stylistic development. Early images have bodies completely covered by thick layers of robes. The robes show prominent folds which give an impression of hardness. The lower hems are arranged in ornamental curves and flare out to the sides. The faces are lively and display a friendly smile. The gaze of images appears to be directed at the viewer. Later images are covered by thin robes which reveal the shape of the body below. The cloth appears to be wet and is clinging to the body. Folds of garments fall in an ornamental rather than natural way. Many robes do not show any folds at all. The gaze is not directed at the viewer but cast down as if the fig.ure were in meditation. This rather dramatic stylistic change parallels the development of Buddhist sculpture in all of Shandong province over the 6th century.

A local characteristic is the extensive use of openwork relief carving. Several fragments belonged to mandorlas or halos that were carved in this way (15.62/no. 22, 15.98/no. 37, C:111/no. 61, C:126). The fragment of a stele shows the body of a dragon that was raised in openwork above the background (C.110/no. 47). This complex and time consuming technique is little known from other temple sites in Shandong.

f) Date of sculptures

Two fragments excavated from the White Dragon site bore dated inscriptions. One damaged inscription on a trias sculpture made of green mica stone contained the characters x泰二年. This should refer to second year of the reign period *putai* 普泰 of the late Northern Wei dynasty, dating the object to 532 AD. A stone base with a long inscription recording a fig.ure donation by two brothers Zhang 張 begins with the dating 大齊天統四年, "4th year of the *tiantong* period of the Great Qi", referring to 568 AD.

Three more fragments with inscribed dates were recovered by Linqu Museum in the vicinity of the site before excavations began. One is the fragment of a mandorla with the engraved characters "Da Wei *xiaochang* ..." 大魏孝昌 .... The precise year is missing but the reign period *xiaochang* lasted from 525 to 527 AD. The fragment of a round halo showed the inscription "*xinghe* er nian" 興和二年, referring to the Eastern Wei and the year 540. A square base with lotos-shaped top recorded the dating x平七年 (seventh year of X-ping) which should refer to period *wuping* 武平 of Northern Qi and the year 576.

Although all sculptures were badly damaged, several can still be dated on stylistic grounds. From the more than 200 fragments, 19 can without doubt be placed into late Northern and Eastern Wei, roughly the years between 525 and 550, while 14 show distinct Northern Qi characteristics and have been made between 550 and 577.

With the exception of one ceramic Buddha image which may have been made during the Tang period, no fragment appears to be of a date later than 600.

g) Condition when found

All images were smashed into small pieces. A few measure about 30 cm on their longest side, but most were broken into much smaller fragments. As some larger fig.ures and steles had a thickness of about 20 cm, they must have suffered considerable force and multiple blows to get broken in this way. Relatively few heads of Buddha or Bodhisattva sculptures survived. In each instance, the head was severed from the torso and the face was smashed. The images were destroyed intentionally and with great zeal.

One fragment of a round halo in the style of the 540s or the Eastern Wei and a second halo fragment of indistinct date showed wedge-shaped recessions on the reverse (216.1/no. 19 and 12.2/no. 39) which points to a secondary repair. No other traces of repairs were found. Since many images found in Longxing Temple in Qingzhou, a temple that had been active for more than 500 years, showed evidence of frequent and repeated repairs (for the repairs of fig.ures from Qingzhou see Lukas Nickel, "Longxing temple in Qingzhou and the discovery of the sculpture hoard", in Lukas Nickel ed., *Return of the Buddha*, Washington 2004, pp. 41–42), the very small number of repair traces on the White Dragon images indicates that the objects had been used for a relatively short period of time only.

Several images retained some traces of pigment and gilding. Most likely all of the sculptures were originally coloured. However, at the time of excavation most fragments had lost all traces of pigments. In addition, the surfaces were in most cases strongly eroded and most of the finer carving was lost. Only few fragments still retained the original polished finishing (15.90/no. 35; C:2, C:3/no. 51). The surfaces of damaged and splintered areas were in most cases strongly eroded and abraded as well, with few sharp edges remaining. This suggests that the fig.ures remained in the open and were exposed to environmental influences for a long period of time after they had been smashed and scattered. One base and foot fragment (C:3/no. 51) sheds further light on this situation. While the skin of the remaining foot and the adjacent areas of the base surface still retain a smooth and polished finish, the broken area on the reverse side is strongly eroded and has lost all sharp edges. This observation indicates that after the object was broken it lay on the ground for a long time, with the remaining foot facing downwards. In this way, the foot area was well preserved while the splintered area weathered. Only much later the object came into the ground.

It is further noteworthy that two fitting fragments of one fig.ure were found at two different locations. The fragment TG304–15:24 (no. 10) was located in a pit to the south of the central terrace and US:1 (no. 11) was placed under the road surface at the bottom of the valley. After their destruction the fig.

ure fragments were apparently dispersed and dumped in different spots on the site. It is likely that the depositions next to the platform and below the street happened at the same time.

Several conclusions can be drawn from the above observations.

The group of stone sculpture fragments found at the White Dragon temple site form a coherent group. The majority is made of the local lime stone and was probably locally produced. One fragment (BK:4/no. 18) found was unfinished, indicating the existence of a carving workshop near the site. Only a few smaller images appear to have been brought here from other fig.ure producing centres. Nearly all were carved in the relatively short time frame of half a century, the period of the late Northern Wei, the Eastern Wei, and Northern Qi dynasties, that is between the 520s and the 570s. This observation concurs with the situation known from Longxing temple in Qingzhou and other temples in the region. Of the about 320 fragmented fig.ures found in Longxing temple, only a hand-full was made after the 6th century. The 6th century was the most active time of fig.ure making and donating in Shandong.

The temple housed a large number of Buddhist images. It included fig.ures made of stone and ceramics, and they were of various sizes. All were originally finely carved and polished as well as painted. Many were gilded. The sculptures follow a distinct stylistic development comparable to the one known from other sites in Shandong province. Even if the White Dragon temple lay in a remote rural area, there is no indication that its images were made in a particularily "provincial" style. They were of high artistic quality. However, on average, the images from Bailong temple appear to have been smaller than the ones known from Longxing temple in the administrative centre Qingzhou.

Only two images showed traces of secondary repairs. This observation differs from the situation in Longxing temple the images of which were in use for nearly 500 years. In this temple, because of the long period of use, most sculptures had been repaired. In some cases, hands or halos had been re-attached repeatedly. We may assume that the images of the White Dragon site had been in use for a limited period of time only.

The fig.ures were severely damaged. All heads were separated from the torsi and smashed, all hands and feet were broken off, and each torso was smashed into several pieces. The fragments are so small that most images must have suffered repeated violent blows. This suggests that the damage was intentional and resulted from violence directed against the images and the temple, rather than from the impact of occasional accidents or an earthquake.

The fig.ure fragments are incomplete. Of most sculptures, only one or two fragments are preserved. Apparently the fig.ures were dispersed and scattered after they were destroyed. Only a part of the fragments were later collected and put into the pits on the site and near the street where they were found. The colours of all images have been washed away, with only few traces remaining. The stone surfaces are strongly weathered and eroded. Obviously the fig.ure fragments lay unprotected in the open for a long time, probably more than one or two centuries, before they were finally placed in pits.

This situation differs from the events as known from Longxing temple in Qingzhou where most images were stored at a well-protected location until the time of interment, even if they had been damaged beyond repair. They were then buried with some ritual procedure in an orderly fashion. At the White Dragon Temple, however, the sculptures were first smashed intentionally and were then left unguarded and unprotected for a long time.

The images of the White Dragon temple were made during the 6th century, beginning in the 520s. The temple continued to exist in the following centuries but there is little evidence of fig.ure-making activity. Since the earliest layer that contained image fragments is layer 70 (70:1 and 70:5/no. 62), the destruction should have taken place at the end of phase 1, in line with the layer 70 horizon. The violent event during which the fig.ures were smashed into pieces and scattered happened during the 9th or 10th centuries. As layer 70 also contained evidence of the sudden collapse of a building one may assume that the iconoclastic event and the destruction of the temple coincide. The image fragments were left without protection from environmental influences for a long time which indicates that the site was not used as a Buddhist temple anymore. The placement of the fig.ures in pits was a secondary event unconnected to the destruction. It took place during phase 3 when the landscape of the area was re-modelled. The event can be dated to the 12th to 13th century.

Final considerations

During the period of political division of China into southern and northern states, the Northern and Southern Dynasties (420–589AD), Shandong area was administered consecutively by the imperial courts of Liu Song, Northern Wei, Eastern Wei, Northern Qi and Northern Zhou. During this period the area experienced the rule of different political regimes and frequent warfare. In a historical environment of social instability and disruption, cultural traditions of various backgrounds began to interact and merge: the traditions of the North and South of China, the traditions of the Han and of other ethnic groups, and the traditions of Chinese and foreign cultures. The climate of clash and renewal became a characteristic of Shandong during the Northern Dynasties. It set the background for a significant development of Confucian, Buddhist and Daoist thought. It became one of the birthplaces of Daoism, a major Chinese religion originating in the mid to late Eastern Han dynasty. Mount Tai and Mount Lao 崂山 became famous places of worship for Daoist monks. Both the Dai Temple 岱庙 of Mount Tai and the Temple of Supreme Purity 太清宫 on Mount Lao are believed to have been built already during the Han period and are still used today.

During the 5th and 6th centuries Buddhism spread all over Shandong. Buddhist sites can be found in almost all areas of the province, with Jinan and Qingzhou as the principle centres. The remains of Buddhist art in Shandong can be divided into four categories: Temple sites, Buddhist caves, rock inscriptions, and independent sculptures (fig. 81).

Most Buddhist temples that were built during in the Northern Dynasties have long been destroyed. Some still exist that are believed to have been established in this period: Lingyan Temple 灵岩寺 and Shentong Temple near Jinan, Fahai Temple 法海寺 on Mount Lao, Baoshou Temple 保寿禅院 on Mount Yungu 云谷山, the Iron Pagoda temple 铁塔寺 in Jining 济宁, Dingling Temple 定林寺 in Fulai Mountain 浮来山, and Puzhao Temple 普照寺 on Mount Tai. Temple sites of the Northern Dynasties that were identified through finds of Buddhist sculptures and stone tablets can be listed as follows: Longxing Temple 龙兴寺 and Xingguo Temple 兴国寺 in Qingzhou, Mingdao Temple 明道寺 and Bailong Temple 白龙寺 in Linqu 临朐, Jinling Temple in Linzi 临淄金陵寺, Longhua Temple 龙华寺 and Xiangyi Temple 乡义寺 in Boxing 博兴, Yongning Temple 永宁寺 in Guangrao 广饶, Shengguo Temple 胜果寺 in Qufu 曲阜, and Yicheng Temple 义城寺 in Juancheng 鄄城. Of the sites mentioned here only Longxing Temple in Qingzhou, Longhua Temple in Boxing as well as the Mingdao and Bailong Temple sites in Linqu have been archaeologically examined so far.

Cave temples and cliff carvings have been found at the Huangshi Cliff 黄石崖 and the Dragon Cave 龙洞 in Jinan, the Lotus Cave 莲花洞 in Changqing, on Sili Mountain 司里山 in Dongping and on Mount Tuo 驼山 in Qingzhou. discovered in Shandong.

Buddhist rock inscriptions can be found mainly in the area between Jinan, Mount Tai and Mount Yi 峄山. The most important ones are the Dragon Cave and the Buddha Valley in Jinan, the Stone Sutra Valley 经石峪 of Mount Tai, Yingxiang Cliff 映像岩 in the Cuilai Mountain 徂徕山 of Xintai 新泰, Buffalo Mountain 水牛山 in Wenshang 汶上, Dahongding Mountain 大洪顶 and Sili Mountain in Dongping, the 'Four Mountains of Zoucheng' – Mount Tie 铁山, Mount Gang 钢山, Mount Ge 葛山, Mount Jian 尖山 – as well as Mount Yi 峄山 and Mount Tao 陶山.

Buddhist sculptures and stele of the 6th century were found in 40 Shandong sites in total. Most concentrate around Qingzhou, Boxing, Zhucheng, Linqu, Linzi and Guangrao. The pit excavated in Longxing Temple contained fragments of at least 320 Buddhist fig.ures made of limestone, marble, granite, terracotta, clay, iron or wood. More than 90% of them were made during the Northern Dynasties period. The Longhua Temple site in Boxing yielded about 100 bronze sculptures of the late 5th and the 6th century. 44 bear inscriptions and 39 contain precise dates in the inscription, offering valuable data about the chronology of Chinese Buddhist bronze sculptures.

Linqu county in particular has always been a centre of Buddhist culture. According to the Ming Dynasty "*Linqu County Chronicle of the Jiaqing period*" 嘉靖临朐县志 of 1552, there were 34 temples. The early *Qing* "*Linqu County Chronicle of the Kangxi period*" 康熙临朐县志 edited in 1672 mentions 60 temples; the "*Linqu County Chronicle of the Guangxu period*" 光绪临朐县志 edited in 1882 lists 19 temples; and the "*Linqu County Local Records of the Guangxu period*" 光绪临朐县乡土志 edited in 1905 mentions more than 30 temples. According to the "*Linqu Continued Chronicle*" 临朐续志 of 1935 there were eight temples in the Republican period.

Linqu county has a broad Buddhist heritage that includes temples, sculptures, cave temples, and rock inscriptions. The most important are the Chongsheng temple 崇圣寺, the Stele in Commemoration of the Rebuilding of the Sanyuan Shrine 三元庙, the Laoyaigu 老崖崮 rock carvings, the Shentanggu 神堂崮 cave temple, the Xiangu Shrine 仙姑庙 , the Waitougu 歪头崮 rock carvings, the Dongzhen Shrine 东镇庙 , the Stone Buddha of the Stone Buddha Hall 石佛堂, the Zhujianchi 铸剑池 stone carvings, and many other sites. The so-far most important Buddhist discovery was made in 1984 when more than 1000 fragments of sculptures of the 6th century were recovered from the foundation of the pagoda of the Mingdao temple site in eastern Linqu.

This excavation brought to light the architectural remains of a rural Buddhist temple that was active between the late Northern Dynasties and the late Tang dynasty. Although the structure was relatively small and the foundations were damaged, the excavation provides scientific data for the study of the development of Buddhism and temple architecture of the Northern Dynasties. For the construction of the temple the area was first levelled. A rectangular platform defined the centre of the structure. Its southern face was in line with the natural terrace border. An artificial ditch bordered the platform to the east, north, and west. Brick walls protected the southern face of the platform and the walls of the ditch. Pathways connected the central platform with the terrace surfaces to the east and west. Under the pathways ran drainage channels that opened to the south. The adjoining terrace surfaces were levelled as well. A small platform was inset into the western border of the ditch. It had a brick paved surface and brick lined borders and was about 90 cm deep. The platform to the north was relatively high. Its surface was not well preserved and its northern border was not found but it measured at least 8 m north to south. South of the central platform there was an entrance situation. A small south facing building stood on the western terrace.

The original buildings on the central and northern platforms were completely destroyed. At the time of excavation no traces of column foundations and or walls remained. The tile and plaster deposits in the ditch suggest that the temple consisted of two main halls aligned on a north-south axis, and a small gravel wall building to the west. Judging from the size of the central and northern platforms and from the number of eve plates of type A and B, it is possible that the building on the central platform was slightly smaller than the one on the northern platform. The halls were traditional wood-post structures with tiled gabled roofs. The walls of the halls were made of clay; they were plastered and to some extent painted. Traces of cold pigment on several eve plates suggest that even the tiles were partly painted. Some of the doors had stone frames and were embellished with large iron nails.

The platform in the north measured about 28 by 8 m. The building erected on it probably was a small to mid-size building. The central platform measured 20 by 15 m, indicating that its building was a small size tile-roofed rectangular building. Judging from the situation in layers 70 and 195 one can assume that at the end of the Tang dynasty, in the 9th to 10th century, the northern building collapsed first, closely followed by the one on the central platform. After that no further temple halls were ever erected again.

The temple was not protected by walls and gates. Northeast of the temple were two brick kilns. The kilns and the discovery of an eve plate mould confirm that the bricks and tiles of the temple were produced locally. Though the temple was located in a remote mountainous area far away from any urban centre, the Buddhist statues excavated exhibit a very high level of craftsmanship. Most images are Buddhist icons made for popular veneration, but some display a rather complex and rarely used iconography. This suggests that the patrons were not just local peasants but came from various strata of society. Many of the sculptures were produced locally, but some had been brought here from other areas. The white buff ceramic bodhisattva figures, for instance, were made with Kaolin earth and most likely come from kilns in the Zibo area in northern Shandong. Many comparable figurines were excavated in the Longhua temple remains in Boxing.

The reason for the destruction of the images and the abandonment of the temple are difficult to establish. All figures were smashed and scattered with intention and zeal at some point during the 9th or 10th century. Literary sources mention a major persecution of the Buddhist and Daoist churches that started in 840. Within a few years 4600 Buddhist and Daoist temples were closed down and their possessions confiscated, more than 260,000 monks and nuns were reconverted to lay men and women, and all temple servants were made commoners. Perhaps the White Dragon Temple was destroyed during this movement, but other reasons for its destruction are possible as well.

The White Dragon temple was established in the early 6th century, probably in the 520s as the earliest inscription provides the date of 525 to 527 AD. Except some grey pottery Buddhist image fragments that may have been made during the Tang dynasty there are no sculpture fragments that were made after 600 AD. The temple remained active throughout the 7th and 8th centuries but the buildings began to slowly dilapidate. At some point in the 9th or 10th century the temple was violently attacked and destroyed and its images were smashed and scattered. After this point the monks abandoned the temple remains and left the figures unguarded and exposed to the environment. Much later, possibly around the 12th and 13th century a new stone faced entrance ramp in the south and several fire places indicate another period of human activity. The surface was remodelled and the remaining figure fragments were collected and disposed of in pits.

Though the temple was located in a remote mountainous area far away from any urban centre, the Buddhist statues excavated exhibit a very high level of craftsmanship. Most images are Buddhist icons made for popular veneration, but some display a rather complex and rarely used iconography. This suggests that the patrons were not just local peasants but came from various strata of society. Many of the sculptures were produced locally, but some had been brought here from other areas. Some eve plates also came from other sites and some of the ceramics were from distant regions. The monks of this temple apparently were in close contact with other Buddhist centres.

Fragments of probably about 100 fig.ures were found. As most fragments have been lost the original number of images in the temple may have been even higher. It is difficult to imagine how such a large number of images may have been displayed and used in such a small temple.

Most sculptures were made during the 6th century. The earliest datable sculptures are of the 520s and the majority was of Eastern Wei or Northern Qi dates. Only a single ceramic fig.ure appears to be of a later date. This small temple was mainly active during the 6th century. However, the presence of a large quantity of ceramic shards and other remains of the Sui and Tang Dynasties and the absence of fig.ure fragments in the lower layers indicate that the buildings continued to exist as a Buddhist temple. Apparently the monks stopped making fig.ures at around the year 600. One needs to ask why the monks and patrons did not continue the established praxis of sculpture donating and making in the seventh and eighth centuries. We hope that future excavations of more Buddhist sites will help solve these questions.

When we began the project of the White Dragon Temple archaeological research on Buddhist sites was still little developed. We hope that the excavation of the site and the publication of the report will provide reliable data for scholarly research, and promote Buddhist archaeology in general.

Postscript

Since we submitted the application for the excavation of the Buddhist site in Xiao Shijiazhuang in 2002, more than a decade has passed and the project went through the stages of excavation, organisation of the materials, documentation and preparation of the publication. For us as the participants of this project the publication of the report is a moment filled with emotions.

In April 1999 workers repairing a street to the side of a small river near the village Xiao Shijiazhuang, found numerous fragments of Buddhist sculptures. The Institute of Archaeology of Shandong Province sent out the archaeologists Li Zhengguang and Hu Changchun 胡常春 to investigate the finds. They concluded that on the slopes of the small valley once had stood a temple of the Northern Dynasties (439–581) (fig. 3) .

In 2001 the Museum Rietberg Zurich in collaboration with the Department of East Asian Art History of Zurich University organised an exhibition that presented the recently recovered Buddhist sculptures from Longxing Temple in Qingzhou, Shandong province, to a Western public for the first time. The exhibition titled "Die Rückkehr des Buddha/The Return of the Buddha" was staged in Zurich, Berlin, and London in 2001 and 2002, and in Washington in 2004. It generated a strong interest in Buddhist sculpture from Shandong among the European public.

In August 2002, Lukas Nickel was invited to China. At the time, Mr. Nickel taught at the Department of East Asian Art History of Zurich University. He had participated in the organisation of the exhibition, and assembled the exhibition catalogue. Mr. Nickel researched Buddhist collections in museums in Qingzhou, Zhucheng, Linqu and other locations and visited the sites of Buddhist temples. In Linqu Museum he came across the fragments discovered in Xiao Shijiazhuang in 1999, and went to see the site together with the vice director of the museum, Gong Dejie 宫德杰. During his visit to the valley near Xiao Shijiazhuang, he formed the idea of organising a joint excavation.

On 2nd September 2002, Mr. Nickel visited the Institute of Archaeology of Shandong Province in the company of Zhang Congjun 张从军, chief of the foreign affairs division of the Shandong Provincial Bureau of Culture, and Zheng Yan 郑岩, deputy director of the Shandong Provincial Museum, where they met the deputy director of the Institute, Tong Peihua. During the meeting, Mr. Nickel proposed a joint excavation of the Buddhist site in Xiao Shijiazhuang. Tong Peihua expressed his willingness to cooperate but raised the need to obtain permission from the Chinese government and the local administrative authorities. Both parties expressed that they would try their best to seek the permissions, assemble a team and obtain funding, and to sign a letter of intent for the joint excavation as soon as possible.

Between October 2002 and March 2003, both parties worked incessantly to secure approval and support from the relevant authorities. The Institute of Archaeology of Shandong Province filed a report to the Shandong Provincial Bureau of Culture and the State Administration of Cultural Heritage and gained recognition. The Department of East Asian Art History obtained funding from the Schweizerisch Liechtensteinische Stiftung für Archäologische Forschungen im Ausland (SLSA). After many rounds of discussions and negotiations, in March 2003 Li Chuanrong, director of the Institute of Archaeology of Shandong Province, and Prof. Dr. Helmut Brinker, head of the Department of East Asian Art History at Zurich University, signed the "Letter of intent for a joint Sino-Swiss project to excavate and research the remains of the White Dragon Temple in Linqu, Shandong" 《关于中瑞合作进行山东临朐白龙寺遗址发掘和研究意向书》 on behalf of the two parties. In May 2003, the Department of East Asian Art History submitted the "Application to the State Administration of Cultural Heritage of China concerning the excavation project of the White Dragon Temple site in Shandong" 《关于山东省白龙寺发掘项目向中国国家文物局呈送的申请》. In June 2003, the Shandong Provincial Bureau of Culture submitted the "Request for instructions concerning the excavation of the White Dragon Temple site in collaboration with Zurich University" 《关于与苏黎世大学联合发掘白龙寺遗址的请示》 to the State Administration of Cultural Heritage.

In late July 2003, in order to obtain the permission from the Chinese government as soon as possible, Tong Peihua, the deputy director of Institute of Archaeology of Shandong Province, accompanied Lukas Schifferle, first secretary of the Swiss embassy to the People's Republic of China, and Lukas Nickel from Zurich University, to visit Song Xinchao 宋新潮, head of the Division for the Protection of Cultural Relics of the State Administration of Cultural Heritage. Mr. Song pointed out that this was the first collaborative project between Switzerland and China in the field of protection of cultural heritage and archaeology, and that the State Administration of Cultural Heritage would give its full support. Mr. Song also gave valuable advice on the forms of collaboration.

In August 2003, the State Administration of Cultural Heritage replied and granted permission for the joint excavation of the White Dragon Temple site. In September 2003, the team consisting of Tong Peihua, Li Zhengguang, Wu Shuangcheng 吴双成 and Gong Dejie on the Chinese side, and Helmut Brinker, Lukas Nickel, Christian Muntwyler, Jorrit Britschgi and Christian Winkel on the Swiss side came together to investigate the site (pl. 2). The Institute of Archaeology of Shandong Province undertook large-scale probings on the northern side of the valley, opened probing trenches, and investigated a small excavation field in order to understand the stratigraphy. The specialists from China and Switzerland exchanged views and discussed in depth the scope of the site and the position of Buddhist relics, and agreed on the excavation methodology and the documentation and drawing standards in preparation for the full excavation in 2004.

In April 2004, the Chinese government fully approved the joint excavation project. Shan Jixiang 单霁翔, director of the State Administration of Cultural Heritage, sent a letter to Helmut Brinker to notify him of the approval and to congratulate for the success of this collaboration in advance. In Switzerland, the Swiss National Science Foundation agreed to fund the work on the project.

In August 2004, the Sino-Swiss team started to fully excavate the Buddhist site of Xiao Shijiazhuang, and extended the probing trenches opened in 2003. The excavated area covered about 1060 m2. In the second year the team was joined by Beat Zollinger and four students from Zurich University: Sue-ling Gremli, Michele Grieder, Geraldine Ramphal, and Thanh Truong (pl. 2.2). The excavation work finished in early October.

In May 2005 the Chinese colleagues led by Li Chuanrong, director of the Archaeological Institute of Shandong Province, visited Zurich University to prepare the documentation and discuss the findings. In 2006 Lukas Nickel, who had by that time taken on a new position at the School of Oriental and African Studies, University of London, and Jorrit Britschgi of Zurich University, joined the Chinese team to work on the documentation, a task that was continued by the Chinese colleagues over the following years. In August and September 2010 Tong Peihua, Li Zhengguang, Wu Shuangcheng, Gong Dejie and Lukas Nickel met again at the working station of the Archaeological Institute of Shandong Province in Linzi, where they finished the documentation and prepared the publication . Tong Peihua, Li Zhengguang, Wu Shuangcheng and Lukas Nickel finalised the Chinese language report during a further working session in October 2014 , after which Lukas Nickel prepared the English part of the book, with support by the SOAS students Wu Hong 吴虹, Ouyang Biqing 欧阳碧晴, and Lin Chun-I 林郡儀. During a final working session in Jinan in August 2015 Tong Peihua, Li Zhengguang and Lukas Nickel prepared the volume for publication.

This project received support and guidance from the Chinese and Swiss governments, as well as from many institutions and experts to all of whom we express our sincere gratitude.

The excavation work was generously funded by the Schweizerisch-Liechtensteinische Stiftung für Archäologische Forschungen im Ausland and the Swiss National Science Foundation. The publication was made possible through funding by the Institute of Archaeology of Shandong Province. We would wish to thank Leica Geosystems for providing a total station, the Commission Suisse pour l'UNESCO and Viamat transport for organising the shipment of the equipment, Nikon Schweiz for providing the camera equipment, and the Swiss Embassy in China, Zurich University, the Kantonsarchäologie Zürich and the Museum Rietberg Zürich for their continuous assistance. The excavations at the White Dragon site were further supported by crowd funding. We wish to thank the Swiss public for its great interest in our work and for backing our enterprise.

We would like to thank the following persons in particular:

Switzerland:

SLSA: Eberhard Fischer

Botschaft der Schweiz in China: Dominique Dreyer, Lukas Schifferle

Museum Rietberg Zürich: Albert Lutz

Commission Suisse pour l'UNESCO: Madeleine Viviani

Leica Geosystems: Fritz Staudacher, Kenneth Li

Kantonsarchäologie Zürich: Andreas Zürcher

VIA MAT Transport: Peter Güttinger

Nikon Schweiz: Pascal Richard

China:

State Administration of Cultural Heritage: Shan Jixiang 单霁翔, Gu Yucai 顾玉才, Song Xinchao 宋新潮, Guan Qiang 关强, Yan Yalin 闫亚林，Tong Wei 佟薇

Peking University: Sun Hua 孙华, Li Chongfeng 李崇峰

Shangdong Provincial Bureau of Culture: Xie Zhixiu 谢治秀, You Shaoping 由少平, Zhang Congjun 张从军

Archaeological Institute of Shandong Province: Zheng Tongxiu 郑同修, Wang Shougong 王守功, Li Chuanrong 李传荣

Shandong Provincial Museum: Lu Wensheng 鲁文生, Zheng Yan 郑岩

Shandong Cultural Relics Scientific Protection Center: Sun Bo 孙博

Weifang City Bureau of Culture: Zhang Baocai 张宝财, Li Guohua 李国华, Tian Yongde 田永德, Miao Qingan 苗庆安

Linqu County Government: Chen Xi 陈曦

Linqu County Bureau of Culture: Liu Chengjie 刘成杰

Linqu County Museum: Sun Bingming 孙秉明, Yi Tongjuan 衣同娟

We thank Si Xiang 司湘 from the Institute of Archaeology of Shandong Province and Lang Fenggang 郎丰刚 from Linqu County Museum for taking charge of the logistics during the excavation period.

Zhang Zhenguo 张振国, Liu Yanchang 刘延常, Zhang Lu 张路, Li Hongliang 李洪亮, Li Shunhua 李顺华, Yan Shengdong 燕生东, Gao Mingkui 高明奎, Lan Yufu 兰玉富, Cui Shengkuan 崔圣宽, Dai

Zunping 戴尊萍 and many other colleagues from the Institute of Archaeology of Shandong Province kindly made all efforts to ensure a smooth success of the collaborative work.

The technicians from the Institute of Archaeology of Shandong Province, Wei Hengchuan 魏恒川, Du Yixin 杜以新, Shi Nianji 石念吉, Sun Liangshen 孙亮慎, Zhang Jingwei 张敬伟, Zhang Shengxian 张圣贤, Li Yuliang 李玉亮 and Wang Tong 王通 worked at the site every day without any break. When important relics were discovered, they also took up the responsibility of guarding the field at night. Yang Jiaxue 杨家学, the skilful cook of the Institute of Archaeology of Shandong Province took care of the meals of the Swiss team. His cooking received praise from all the scholars. We thank all of them for their efforts!

This report is the result of the collaborative work of the joint team from China and Switzerland. The report was written by the following people:

Preface: Xie Zhixiu 谢治秀

Chapter 1: Tong Peihua 佟佩华, Gong Dejie 宫德杰, Wu Shuangcheng 吴双成

Chapter 2: Tong Peihua 佟佩华

Chapter 3: Tong Peihua 佟佩华

Chapter 4: Li Zhenguang 李振光

Chapter 5: Li Zhenguang 李振光

Chapter 6: Li Zhenguang 李振光, Lukas Nickel

Chapter 7: Li Zhenguang 李振光, Lukas Nickel

Chapter 8: Lukas Nickel, Li Zhenguang 李振光

Postscript: Tong Peihua 佟佩华, Lukas Nickel

English version: Lukas Nickel

Surveying and mapping with total station: Christan Muntwyler, Beat Zollinger, Christian Winkel

Photography: Wu Shuangcheng 吴双成, Jorrit Britschgi, Lukas Nickel

Assembly of maps: Wu Shuangcheng 吴双成

Drawings: Zhang Yingjun 张英军, Wang Zhanqin 王站琴

Rubbings: Gong Dejie 宫德杰

The members of the joint excavation team were:

Chinese side: Tong Peihua, Li Zhengguang, Wu Shangcheng and Gong Dejie

Swiss side: Helmut Brinker, Lukas Nickel, Christian Muntwyler, Jorrit Britschgi, Beat Zollinger and Chistian Winkel.

后 记

山东临朐小时家庄佛家遗址发掘从2002年立项申报开始，经历考古调查发掘、资料整理、撰写编辑和出版发行几个阶段，一晃走过了十余个年头。我们做为这个项目的具体执行人，心中自有说不尽的感慨。

2001年中国青州龙兴寺佛教窖藏造像大展在德国柏林、瑞士苏黎世和英国伦敦进行巡展，引起了欧洲史学界、考古界和美术界的广泛关注。

2002年8月，参加瑞士苏黎世中国青州龙兴寺窖藏佛造像大展筹备工作，并编辑出版展览图录的瑞士苏黎世大学东亚美术史系教师倪克鲁先生应邀来到中国。倪克鲁先生先后参观了青州、诸城和临朐等地博物馆馆藏佛造像，并到一些佛教寺院遗址进行了现场考察，在考察临朐县石家河乡小时家庄佛教遗址时，萌发了通过中国山东省考古研究机构合作发掘该遗址的大胆设想。

2002年9月2日，倪克鲁先生在山东省文化厅外事处处长张从军先生和山东省博物馆副馆长郑岩先生陪同下，到山东省文物考古研究所进行参观访问，山东省文物考古研究所副所长佟佩华先生接待了倪克鲁先生一行。在双方交谈中，倪克鲁先生提出中瑞双方合作发掘临朐小时家庄佛教遗址的建议。佟佩华先生表示愿意同瑞方合作，同时也提出中瑞合作需要经中国政府批准，要向省文物主管部门报告。双方表示，要尽最大努力落实人员、经费和报批等问题，尽早签署中瑞合作发掘临朐小时家庄佛教遗址意向书。

2002年10月至2003年3月间，中、瑞双方积极努力争取了主管部门和相关单位的支持。山东省文物考古研究所先后向山东省文化厅和国家文物局做了汇报，得到认可。苏黎世大学东亚美术史系也争取到Schweizerisch Liechtensteinische Stiftung für Archäologische Forschungen im Ausland（SLSA）基金会的资助。通过多次沟通和协商，2003年3月，山东省文物考古研究所所长李传荣研究员和瑞士苏黎世大学东亚美术史系主任布伦克教授（Prof. Dr. Helmut H. Brinker）分别代表中瑞双方签署了《关于中瑞合作进行山东临朐白龙寺遗址发掘和研究意向书》。2003年5月，瑞士苏黎世大学东亚美术史系向国家文物局提交了《关于山东省白龙寺发掘项目向中国国家文物局呈送的申请》。2003年6月，山东省文化厅向国家文物局报送了《关于与苏黎世大学联合发掘白龙寺遗址的请示》报告。

为了尽早得到中国政府的批准，2003年7月30日，山东省文物考古研究所副所长佟佩华先生陪同瑞士王国驻中华人民共和国大使一等秘书 Lukas Schifferle 先生和瑞士苏黎世大学东亚美术史系倪克鲁先生到国家文物局拜会国家文物局文物保护司负责人宋新潮先生。宋先生指出，这是中瑞双方在文物保护和发掘领域的第一个合作项目，国家文物局全力支持，并就合作的具体形式提出了很好的建议。

2003年8月，国家文物局批复，同意瑞士苏黎世大学考古学者参观临朐白龙寺遗址发掘工地。2003年9月，山东省文物考古研究所在临朐小时家庄进行勘探，并开挖探沟了解遗址地层堆积情况。中瑞专家就遗址范围、佛教遗存位置进行了深入的交流和探讨，并就发掘方法、记录方式和绘图规范达成共识，为2004年正式发掘做了准备。

2004年4月，中国政府批准了中瑞合作发掘临朐白龙寺遗址项目。中国国家文物局局长单霁翔致函瑞士苏黎世大学东亚美术史系主任布伦克教授，告知中国政府批准之事，并预祝合作圆满成功。

2004年8月，中瑞考古队正式在临朐小时家庄佛教遗址进行发掘，发掘面积1160平方米，发掘工作至10月上旬结束。

本项目得到中瑞两国政府和许多专家的支持和指导，在此一并表示感谢。

瑞士方面：

瑞士和列支敦士登国外考古学研究基金会 （SLSA）：Eberhard Fischer

瑞士驻华使馆：H. E. Mr. Dominique Dreyer, Lukas Schifferle

Museum Rietberg Zürich: Albert Lutz

Commission Suisse pour l'UNESCO: Madeleine Viviani

Leica Geosystems: Fritz Staudacher, Kenneth Li

Kantonsarchäologie Zürich: Andreas Zürcher

VIA MAT Transport: Peter Güttinger

Nikon Schweiz: Pascal Richard

中国方面：

国家文物局：单霁翔、顾玉才、宋新潮、关强、闫亚林、佟薇

北京大学：孙华、李崇峰

山东省文化厅：谢治秀、由少平、张从军

山东省文物考古研究所：郑同修、王守功、李传荣

山东省博物馆：鲁文生、郑岩

山东省文物科技保护中心：孙博

潍坊市文化局：张宝财、李国华、田永德、苗庆安

临朐县人民政府：陈曦

临朐县文化局：刘成杰

临朐县博物馆：孙秉明、衣同娟

在2003年和2004年发掘期间，山东省文物考古研究所司湘先生和临朐县博物馆郎丰刚先生承担了繁重的后勤保障工作。

在合作期间，山东省文物考古研究所张振国、刘延常、张路、李洪亮、李顺华、燕生东、高明奎、兰玉富、崔圣宽、戴尊萍等人付出了大量心血。

在发掘期间，山东省文物考古研究所技工魏恒川、杜以新、石念吉、孙亮慎、张敬伟、张圣贤、李玉亮、王通等冒酷暑始终坚守在发掘一线。发现重要文物后，他们又承担了工地夜间值班保卫的任务。山东省文物考古研究所厨师杨家学心灵手巧，根据瑞士学者的口味和需要，不断烹饪出可口的饭菜，得到瑞士学者的好评。我们向他们表示感谢！

中瑞临朐小时家庄白龙寺联合考古队名单：中国：佟佩华、李振光、吴双成、宫德杰。瑞士：布伦克、倪克鲁、孟为乐、贝昱瑞、毕亚特、温克。

本报告是中瑞双方合作的结晶，具体报告撰写分工是：

第一章：佟佩华

第二章：宫德杰、吴双成

第三章：佟佩华

第四章：李振光

第五章：李振光

第六章：李振光、倪克鲁

第七章：李振光、倪克鲁

第八章：倪克鲁、李振光

后记：佟佩华

英文报告：倪克鲁

全站仪测绘：孟为乐、毕亚特、温克

照相：吴双成、贝昱瑞、倪克鲁

图片合成：吴双成

绘图：张英军、王站琴

拓片：宫德杰

编　者

彩　版

1. 临朐白龙寺遗址自然环境（东向西）

2. 临朐白龙寺遗址发掘前遗址面貌

彩版一（pl.1） 临朐白龙寺遗址

1. 发掘人员合影（从左向右：孟为乐、佟佩华、布伦克、倪克鲁、贝昱瑞、李振光、宫德杰）

2. 发掘人员合影（从左向右：孙秉明、贝昱瑞、佟佩华、刘成杰、布伦克、李传荣、倪克鲁、毕亚特、孟为乐、李振光、宫德杰）

彩版二（pl.2）　白龙寺遗址工作照

1．2004年工作场景（从西向东）

2．现场讨论

彩版三（pl.3）　白龙寺遗址工作照

1. 2006年在临淄工作站整理报告

2. 2014年讨论定稿

彩版四（pl.4） 白龙寺遗址工作照

1. 全站仪测绘

2. 设立测绘基点之一（从东南向西北）

彩版五（pl.5） 野外测绘

1. 设立测绘基点之二（从南向北）

2. 标牌标识探方位置

彩版六（pl.6） 野外测绘

1. 方格网绘图

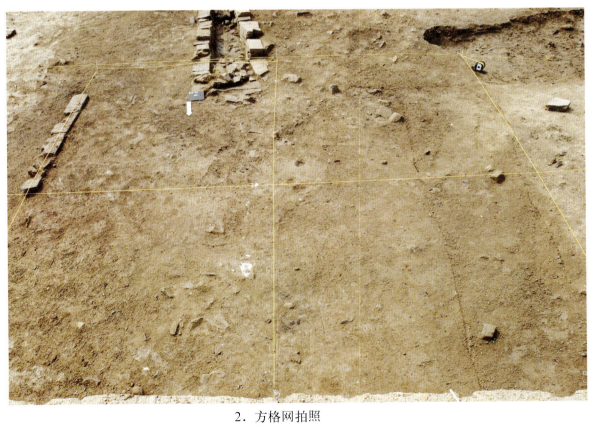

2. 方格网拍照

彩版七（pl.7） 野外测绘

1. 一米方格网绘图

2. 全站仪测绘之三

彩版八（pl.8） 野外测绘

1．瑞士考古专用绘图纸

2．测绘标图

彩版九（pl.9） 绘图

1. 绘制图纸

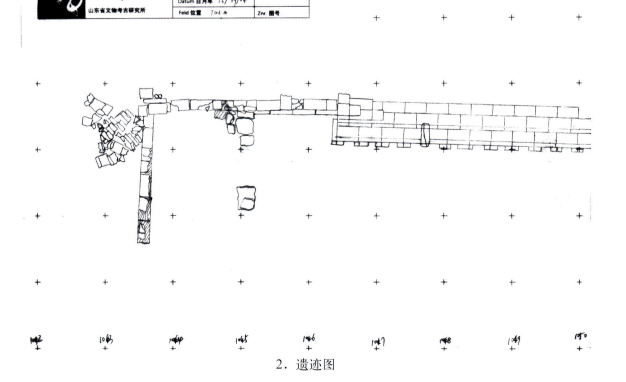

2. 遗迹图

彩版一〇（pl.10） 绘图

1. 设置标志照相

2. 设标志点

彩版一一（pl.11） 野外测绘

1. 登高照相

2. 手铲

彩版一二（pl.12） 白龙寺遗址工作照

1．T424西壁剖面（从东向西）

2．T423、433东壁剖面

3．T424、434西壁剖面（从东向西）

彩版一三（pl.13） 探方剖面

1. 建筑基址全景（从南向北）

2. 建筑基址全景（从北向南）

彩版一四（pl.14） 建筑基址全景

1. 建筑基址全景（从东向西）

2. 建筑基址全景（从西向东）

彩版一五（pl.15） 建筑基址全景

1. 长方形台基南侧砖墙（从东南向西北）

2. 长方形台基南侧砖墙局部（从南向北）

3. 长方形台基南侧砖墙顶视

彩版一六（pl.16） 长方形台基

1. 长方形台基北侧砖墙（从西北向东南）

2. 长方形台基北侧砖墙（从北向南）

彩版一七（pl.17） 长方形台基

1. 长方形台基西墙基槽

2. 长方形台基西墙基础

彩版一八（pl.18） 长方形台基

1. 西侧慢道、排水口外砖墙（从南向北）

2. 西侧排水沟槽上部盖板（从上向下）

彩版一九（pl.19）　西侧慢道与排水沟槽

1. 西侧排水沟槽上部盖板（从上向下）

2. 西侧排水沟槽（从上向下）

彩版二〇（pl.20） 西侧排水沟槽

1. 东侧排水沟槽与前侧砖墙（从南向北）

2. 东侧排水沟槽

3. 东侧排水沟槽

彩版二一（pl.21）　东侧排水沟槽

1．T423—433堆积64

2．T434堆积64

彩版二二（pl.22） 堆积64分布

1. 内庭地面

2. 堆积195

彩版二三（pl.23） 内庭地面与堆积195

1. 北侧高台砖墙（从东南向西北）

2. 北侧高台砖墙（从南向北）

彩版二四（pl.24） 北侧高台砖墙

1．西侧高台砖墙（从东向西）

2．西侧高台砖墙（从东南向西北）

3．西侧高台砖墙局部

彩版二五（pl.25） 西侧高台砖墙

1. 南侧通道（从南向北）

2. 早期通道东侧砖墙（从东向西）

彩版二六（pl.26） 南侧通道

1．中期通道东侧护坡砖墙（堆积165，从东向西）

2．中期通道西侧护坡砖墙（堆积166）

彩版二七（pl.27）　南侧通道护坡砖墙

1. 晚期通道西侧护坡石墙（堆积74，从西向东）

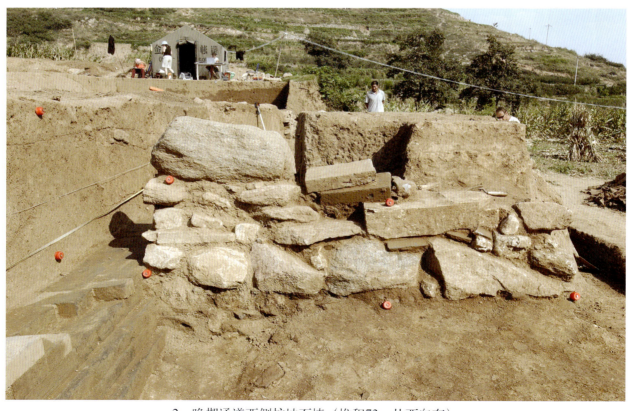

2. 晚期通道西侧护坡石墙（堆积73，从西向东）

彩版二八（pl.28） 晚期通道西侧护坡石墙

1．小房子倒塌堆积

2．小房子（从南向北）

3．小房子北墙（从南向北）

彩版二九（pl.29） 小房子

1. 陶窑（从南向北）

2. 陶窑（从南向北）

彩版三〇 （pl.30） 陶窑

1. 陶窑（从西向东）

2. 陶窑窑柱（从南向北）

彩版三一（pl.31） 陶窑

1. 白灰墙壁

2. 造像瓦当出土场景

彩版三二（pl.32） 遗物出土情况

1. Z122

2. Z152

3. Z152

彩版三三（pl.33） 烧灶

1. 墓葬盖板

2. 墓葬内埋葬情况

3. 墓葬出土瓷罐

4. 墓葬出土瓷灯

彩版三四（pl.34） 墓葬及出土瓷器

1. 筒瓦T434-195：1

2. 筒瓦T434-195：1

3. 筒瓦T434-195：1

4. 板瓦T425-64：3

5. 板瓦T425-64：3

彩版三五（pl.35） 出土陶瓦

1．A型瓦当TG1-15：8

2．A型瓦当堆积64：4

3．A型瓦当堆积64：7

4．A型瓦当内模TG1-15：25

5．B型瓦当T434-70：15

6．C型瓦当T433-68：2

彩版三六（pl.36） 出土瓦当

1. B型瓦当04XL200-201：4

2. B型瓦当04XL200-201：4

3. D型瓦当TG1-5：1

4. E型瓦当T413-178：5

5. F型瓦当T434-64：1

彩版三七（pl.37） 出土瓦当

1. F型瓦当T434—70：17

2. F型瓦当T434—70：17

3. F型瓦当T434—70：17

4. F型瓦当T434—70：17

彩版三八（pl.38） 出土瓦当

1．Aa型瓷碗TG204−5：1

2．Aa型瓷碗TG204−5：1

3．Aa型瓷碗T434−5：4

4．Aa型瓷碗T434−70：3

5．Aa型瓷碗T434−70：3

6．Aa型瓷碗T435−238：5

彩版三九（pl.39） 出土瓷碗

1．Ab型瓷碗T413-179：12

2．Ab型瓷碗T413-179：12

3．Ba型瓷碗T434-68：2

4．Ba型瓷碗T434-68：2

5．Ba型瓷碗T434-198：5

6．Ba型瓷碗T434-198：5

彩版四○（pl.40）　出土瓷碗

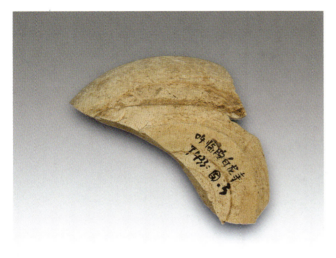

1. Ba型瓷碗T433-5：3

2. Bb型瓷碗T433-5：2

3. Bb型瓷碗T434-69：103

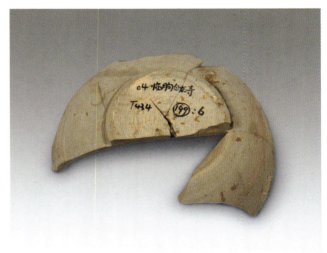

4. Bc型瓷碗T434-199：6

5. Bc型瓷碗T434-199：6

6. Bc型瓷碗T434-199：6

彩版四一（pl.41） 出土瓷碗

1．Bc型瓷碗T434-64：13

2．Bc型瓷碗T434-64：13

3．C型瓷碗T423-69：101

4．C型瓷碗T414-174：1

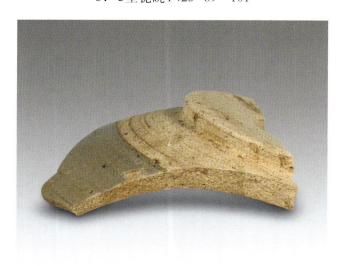

5．C型瓷碗T414-174：1

彩版四二（pl.42） 出土瓷碗

1. C型瓷碗T413-178：7

2. C型瓷碗T413-178：7

3. C型瓷碗T425-195：15

4. C型瓷碗T425-195：15

5. C型瓷碗T423-117：2

6. C型瓷碗T423-117：2

彩版四三（pl.43） 出土瓷碗

1．D型瓷碗T434-68：7

2．瓷碗T434-68：17

3．瓷碗T434-64：124

4．瓷碗T434-5：3

5．瓷碗T435-70：18

1. A型瓷钵T434-198：1

2. A型瓷钵T434-198：1

3. A型瓷钵T434-198：1

彩版四五（pl.45）　出土瓷钵

1．B型瓷钵T433-70：19

2．B型瓷钵T433-70：19

3．B型瓷钵T435-238：6

4．B型瓷钵T435-238：6

彩版四六（pl.46）　出土瓷钵

1. 瓷罐T413—BK：4

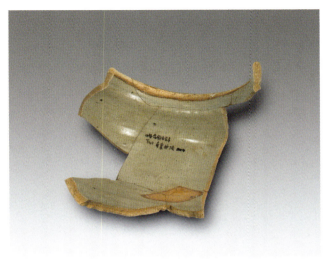

2. 瓷罐T413—BK：4

3. 瓷罐T433—5：1

4. 瓷罐T433—5：1

5. 瓷罐T433—118：4

6. 瓷罐T433—118：4

彩版四七（pl.47）　出土瓷罐

1. A型瓷罐底T433-70：20

2. A型瓷罐底T433-70：20

3. A型瓷罐底T433-70：20

4. B型瓷罐底T434-68：15

5. B型瓷罐底T434-68：15

6. B型瓷罐底T434-68：15

彩版四八（pl.48） 出土瓷罐底

1. 瓷壶口T423-69：109

2. 黑瓷壶T435-195：13

3. 黑瓷壶T434-198：8

4. 瓷壶T425-70：5

5. 瓷壶T425-70：5

彩版四九（pl.49） 出土瓷壶

1. 瓷壶T434-64：17

2. 瓷壶T434-64：17

3. 瓷壶T434-64：17

4. 瓷壶T434-64：17

彩版五〇（pl.50）　出土瓷壶

1. 三彩瓷豆柄T434-64：14

2. 三彩瓷豆柄T434-64：14

3. 三彩瓷豆柄T434-64：14

4. 三彩瓷豆柄T434-64：14

5. 三彩瓷豆柄T434-64：14

6. 三彩瓷豆柄T434-64：14

彩版五一（pl.51） 出土三彩瓷豆柄

1. 铜钩TG203-29：1

2. 铜耳勺T434-68：1

3. 五铢TG105-15：13

4. 五铢TG105-15：13

5. 开元通宝T434-68：1

6. 乾元重宝T434-1：1

彩版五二（pl.52） 出土铜器与铜钱

1. 骨锥T434—70∶13

2. 骨锥T434—70∶13

3. 鹿角T423—118∶3

4. 鹿角T423—118∶3

5. 鹿角T423—118∶1

6. 鹿角T423—118∶1

彩版五三（pl.53） 出土骨器与鹿角

1. 石造像TG3-15：17

3. 石造像TG3-15：13

2. 石造像TG3-15：17

4. 石造像TG3-15：13

彩版五四（pl.54）　出土石造像

1．石造像TG304−15：56、15

2．石造像TG304−15：69、70

3．石造像TG304−15：16

4．石造像TG304−15：84

5．石造像TG304−15：35

彩版五五（pl.55）　出土石造像

1. 石造像TG304-15：14

2. 石造像TG105-15：6

3. 石造像TG105-15：6

彩版五六（pl.56） 出土石造像

1．石造像TG105-15：73

2．石造像TG304-15：34

3．石造像TG304-15：62

4．石造像TG304-15：23

5．石造像TG304-15：81

6．石造像T414-BK：4

彩版五七（pl.57） 出土石造像

1．石造像TG304—15：49

2．石造像TG304—15：24

3．石造像路基US：1

4．石造像TG304—15：4

5．石造像TG304—15：45

6．石造像TG304—15：65

彩版五八（pl.58） 出土石造像

1. 石造像TG304—15：90

2. 石造像TG204—15：79

3. 石造像TG304—15：28

4. 石造像TG105—15：5

5. 石造像TG304—15：77

6. 石造像TG304—15：77

彩版五九（pl.59）　出土石造像

1. 石造像TG202－216：1　　　2. 石造像TG202－217：1　　　3. 石造像TG202－217：1

4. 石造像TG304－15：33　　　5. 石造像T434－69：1　　　6. 石造像T434－69：1

7. 石造像T434－69：1　　　8. 石造像TG304－56、57：1　　　9. 石造像TG305－58：2

1. 石造像TG305-58：1　　2. 石造像TG305-58：1　　3. 石造像T413-178：2

4. 石造像T414-12：2　　5. 石造像T414-12：2　　6. 石造像T413-BK：1

7. 石造像T413-BK：1　　8. 石造像T414-12：1　　9. 石造像T414-12：1

彩版六一（pl.61）　出土石造像

1. 白陶造像T413−70：5

2. 白陶造像T414−74：2

4. 白陶造像TG304—C：1

3. 灰陶造像T434−201：6

5. 白陶造像T413−181：4

彩版六二（pl.62）　出土陶造像

1. 石造像C：1

2. 石造像C：1

3. 石造像C：101

4. 石造像C：123

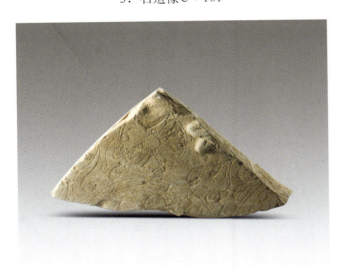

5. 石造像C：123

6. 石造像C：125

彩版六三（pl.63） 出土石造像

1. 石造像C：115

2. 石造像C：115

3. 石造像C：115

4. 石造像C：114

5. 石造像C：117

6. 石造像C：117

彩版六四（pl.64）　出土石造像

1．石造像C：122

2．石造像C：122

3．石造像C：110

4．石造像C：121

5．石造像C：124

彩版六五（pl.65） 出土石造像

1. 石造像C：120

2. 石造像C：120

3. 石造像C：120

4. 石造像C：109

5. 石造像C：109

彩版六六（pl.66） 出土石造像

1. 石造像C：116

2. 石造像C：116

3. 石造像C：108

4. 石造像C：111

5. 石造像C：118

6. 石造像C：107

彩版六七（pl.67） 出土石造像